BELIEF UNBOUND

BELIEF UNBOUND

A PROMETHEAN RELIGION FOR THE MODERN WORLD

BY

WM. PEPPERELL MONTAGUE

PROFESSOR OF PHILOSOPHY, COLUMBIA UNIVERSITY

NEW HAVEN · YALE UNIVERSITY PRESS

LONDON · HUMPHREY MILFORD · OXFORD UNIVERSITY PRESS

TO

W. P. M., Jʀ.

CONTENTS

I

THE MODERN CHALLENGE TO
THE OLD RELIGION

THAT confused and many-sided thing, characterized by Mr. Krutch as "the modern temper," is challenging the old religion; and this challenge is more self-assured, more varied, and in all ways more momentous than any with which religion has been confronted in the past. Every religion, and particularly a great historic faith such as Christianity, is a mixture of physics and ethics, a transcendental or metaphysical physics and an authoritarian and impassioned ethics. And the modern challenge to religion is a twofold thing; it attacks both the religious conception of nature and the religious conception of human values and ideals.

Now I believe that the current attacks upon religion contain much that is metaphysically sound and morally healthy together with much that is fallacious and deplorable. But quite apart from their logical validity the antireligious arguments possess a psychological strength that is due to their profound congruity with modern moods and tempers. It is because of this congruity with the general spirit of the time that the movement against religion is steadily and rapidly increasing in influence. And for perhaps the first time in history we are confronted with the prospect of a complete secularization of the opinions, the practices, and the emotions of mankind. There are of course many forces operating against this tendency. Not only are there the various flare-ups of Fundamentalism and militant orthodoxy of all kinds, but there are the still more numerous compromises of Modernism. These latter range all the way from the mildly rationalized forms of Broad Church Episcopalianism through traditional Unitarianism to the faintly devout Naturalism of those who would reduce Divinity to whatever factors of the environment are conducive to the good life. I cannot but feel, however, that in most of these compromises the gains in reasonableness and scientific plausibility hardly compensate for the loss in emotional intensity. Religion as the experience of the supernatural is an all-or-none kind of thing. To try for a genteel modicum of it is like hitting soft.

There is, it seems to me, a quite different way of meeting the situation, a way that involves a revolutionary reorientation of religion and a radical reinterpretation of the supernatural and of its relation to us. And there is a possibility that by such a revolution the decline of religion may be checked and the idea of God be given a new and more secure place in the lives of men.

The object of these chapters is to consider the objections to religion as it is, and to outline a conception of religion as it might be if subjected to the reconstruction just mentioned.

The environment of a man upon adjustment to which his weal and woe depend is a twofold affair.

It contains things and it contains persons. The technique of adjustment to things is *compulsion;* the technique of adjustment to persons is not merely compulsion but, and more especially, *persuasion.* From the one technique develops science, from the other, the arts and institutions of social life—in a word, culture. Now to all, or most, of the primitive peoples and to many, if not most, of those who are civilized, the visible environment is supplemented by an environment that is invisible and supernatural. This secondary environment resembles its primary counterpart in containing both persons and things, and in requiring the technique of persuasion for adjusting to the former and of compulsion for adjusting to the latter. There thus enter into the domain of human concerns two shadowy extensions of our natural intercourse with the natural world: first, Religion, the unearthly supplement to the association of mortals with mortals, second, Magic, the dark sister of science. But between persons and things, whether natural or supernatural, there is of course no absolute cleavage, and the religious technique of moral persuasion and the magical technique of physical compulsion can be mixed in all sorts of ways. One and the same community may contain not only priests and wizards, but shamans exercising the functions of both.

In its earlier stages religion seems to consist largely of the attempts of men to adapt themselves to a multitude of capricious and demon-like beings and to the mysterious forces associated with them. But as religion develops the gods become fewer and better. The discovery of natural causes for natural phenomena renders the adjustment to supernatural causes superfluous. Magic becomes permeated by science and religion takes on moral meaning. And from the crowded pantheons of primitive culture we pass to highly select aristocracies like those of Mount Olympus, composed of a blend of racial heroes and personified natural powers. From such a polytheism it is but a step to monotheism, in which a Yahweh, ceasing to be a merely tribal deity, takes on the dignity of a world creator and a Zeus, usurping more and more of the specialized functions of his cabinet ministers, evolves from a constitutional monarch to an absolute dictator. More important than the diminishing numbers of the divinities is their improvement in character. Each new grace and virtue disclosed by the maturing human conscience is conferred upon the gods above. They cease to be merely capricious and demonic and become repositories of human values, embodiments of goodness and righteousness. This later ethical aspect of divinity can indeed quite overshadow the earlier physical characteristics, so that the object of religion may be conceived as an immaterial spirit, or as an impersonal principle of justice objectified in the structure of the universe, like the Buddhist Karma, or as a realm of blessed and purified being, such as Nirvana.

There are two further and quite recent stages in the development of religion. In one of them the reference to an objective existence drops out altogether. Divinity ceases to be thought of as an actuality and is employed as a symbol for our highest values and ideals. The name God, if still used, is used only as a dramatic name for the good, and religion becomes "morality touched with emotion." The old liturgies and rituals, to the extent that they are retained, are justified as a poetry of the spirit and are, like other poetry, held innocent of existential truth. The other of the recent developments of religion is opposite in nature to the one of which we have just spoken. Instead of God being conceived as nothing but an ideal, lacking objective existence, he is thought of as nothing but the ultimate reality, the source and ground of nature. Religion then becomes the recognition of this Absolute and the adjustment of our lives to its laws. Now in view of the bewilderingly heterogeneous denotation of the term "religion," the problem of discovering a single connotation or definition is a difficult one. What nucleus of meaning can we find that is common to the essentially non-theistic Buddhism, to Christian theism, and to those mixtures of magical practice and the placation of demons which constitute many of the religions of primitive culture? And if to these earlier uses of the term "religion" we add the looser usages of the present day, in which the word "religion" may designate a purely humanistic devotion to this or that ideal of social living or a purely pantheistic experience of the mystery or majesty or lawfulness of the cosmos, the problem of definition seems insoluble. If we insist that the definition shall be precisely equivalent to the thing defined, we may at best arrive at some merely formal or extrinsic and insignificant characteristic. If, on the other hand, we insist upon an attribute possessing essentiality we shall probably be unable to fit that connotation to all the cases denoted by the term. I believe that the latter failure is the lesser evil, and that we should be content to seek a unified meaning for those instances of the concept which are most important in themselves and most relevant to the purpose for which the definition is sought.

One such meaning of Religion there is; and from the welter of usages it leaps out to meet us and challenge our minds and our hearts. It is the meaning that applies neither to the primitive nor to the sophisticated instances of religion. Religion as we shall use the term is not a traffic with demons and the dark forces pertaining to them. The belief in such objects is almost certainly false and quite certainly without moral significance. Nor is religion merely a belief in an ultimate reality or in an ultimate ideal. These beliefs are worse than false; they are platitudes, truisms, that nobody will dispute. Religion as we shall conceive it is the acceptance neither of a primitive absurdity nor of a sophisticated truism, but of a momentous possibility—the possibility namely that what is highest in spirit is also deepest in nature, that the ideal and the real are at least to some extent identified, not merely evanescently in our own lives but enduringly in the universe itself. If this possibility were an actuality, if there truly were at the heart of nature something akin to us, a conserver and increaser of values, and if we could not only know this and act upon it, but really feel it, life would suddenly become radiant. For no longer should we be alien accidents in an indifferent world, uncharacteristic by-products of the blindly whirling atoms; and no longer would the things that matter most be at the mercy of the things that matter least.

When we raise the question of the truth of religion, it is this momentous possibility that is at stake. We have a great hope shadowed by a great fear. The fear is that the belief in a cosmic power for good may have no other grounds than the yearning of cowering human hearts, and that the voice of God which has so often been heard may be no more than man's own cry mockingly echoed back to him by the encompassing void.

It is because of the momentousness of the issue that it is something worse than disappointing to find a great scientist cheerfully reassuring his readers that there is no conflict between religion and science, on the ground that the latter contains nothing that is opposed to the Christian ideals of justice and charity. As though anyone had ever made the claim that is here triumphantly denied. Religion is a eulogistic term, and many who have lost their faith in it, in any sense in which it matters, will cling lovingly to the word and use it as a designation for a devotion to their favorite ethical ideals. And quite analogously those who no longer believe in any existent divinity will fight like tigers against the supposedly derogatory appellations of "atheistic" and "irreligious."

When affection or disaffection for words is permitted to override their meanings, the wells of discourse are muddied and there ensues no advantage either ethical or logical.

The religion that is under attack today is not religion in its paltry and vaguely eulogistic sense; it is religion as we defined it—the faith that there is in nature an urge or power other than man himself that makes for the kind of thing that man regards as good. When we survey the antireligious arguments, we find them directed against the generic essence of any religion and also against the details of particular religions such as Christianity. The general and special lines of attack are, moreover, by no means kept separate by those who use them; and the manner in which they are blended together makes their analysis and appraisal most difficult. The phases of Christianity that appear most repugnant to the modern temper are, first, its methodology of Authoritarianism; second, its ethics of Asceticism and Other-worldliness; third, its metaphysics of Supernaturalism. Let us consider these in turn.

Authoritarianism.

In any human group, the ancient Jewish people, for example, there develops a folklore which is the composite resultant of those individual attitudes, sentiments, and beliefs, which by a kind of natural selection have survived as the apparently fittest in the minds of the tribe and its leaders. The growing body of folklore contains not only ways of behavior but ways of belief about behavior and about the world.

These dominant systems of beliefs about what ought to be and what is, constitute the ethics and the physics of the group. With the development of those beliefs there will naturally develop a group within the group whose special business it is to guard and transmit the tribal wisdom. These guardians or priests, usually the elders of the people, would be more than human if they did not become attached to the wisdom which gives them occupation and honor. They would also be more than human if their devotion were not intensified and their loyalty hardened by any threat of rivalry on the part of new secular beliefs in conflict with their own customary ones. And they would be more than primitive if they did not tend to give additional prestige to their beliefs (especially when the natural or human origins of those beliefs have been forgotten) by ascribing them more and more to the revelation of supernatural powers, on whose authority they are to be accepted without question. *There thus ensues a strange phenomenon, perhaps the strangest and the most retrogressive in all human culture, which consists in the translation of the crude hypotheses of our ignorant ancestors into dogmas proclaimed by divine omniscience.* When a folkway or hypothesis once becomes promoted to the status of a dogma, it becomes sacrosanct, unamendable, and immune to all criticism. The men of later generations must live under the dead hand of their ancestral past, and no matter what new discoveries are made about the nature of the world, and no matter to what extent changes in the conditions of life may cry out for changes in the rules of living, the supposedly divine dispensation must not be altered.

The Christian Bible is just such a body of folklore as we have been describing. It is composed of the beliefs held by the ancient Jews and the early Christians, some of them ugly, cruel, and absurdly false, others beautiful, just, and true, all of them mixed together and construed as a divine revelation to which all later human science and philosophy must be made to accord on pain of being in error.

This is the primary phase of that authoritarianism with which Christianity, like the other great religions, is so profoundly imbued. But there are two derivative phases that are almost as important.

The first of these derivatives of authoritarianism is the invention of the pseudo-sin of Heresy and the pseudo-virtue of Orthodoxy. If you dissent from the ancestral hypotheses you not only suffer the misfortune of being in error, but you are, in addition, committing a wrong for which you should be punished; while, correspondingly, if you accept the ancient creed, you not only enjoy the good fortune of seeing the light but you are deserving of moral credit. It is only because long familiarity has dulled our discrimination, that the preposterousness of such evaluations is not recognized. Suppose that a religious creed were actually true and that it had come from God himself. To blame a person for a failure to realize its truth, would be like blaming a blind man for his blindness. It is not blame, but a great pity and a

will to help, that should be felt by the Orthodox
for the Heterodox. And instead of taking credit to
themselves for their own good fortune in being vouch-
safed the vision of truth, they should feel especially
humble, and especially obligated to live more nobly
than their less favored brothers. One need not drag
up the uncounted agonies inflicted by the true be-
lievers upon those who could not truly believe. There
would be shame enough to the Church even if it had
been guiltless of actual persecution, in its harboring
the idea that the boon of knowing God's truth was
a virtue and the lack of that knowledge a sin.

The other evil product of the authoritarian spirit
is its implicit yet thoroughgoing subordination of
what ought to be to what is, of value to fact, of right
to might, of ethics to religion. It gives us a morality
of commands and taboos, instead of a morality of
ideals; it makes goodness consist in conforming to
the powers that be rather than in adapting those
powers to the requirements of ideal beauty and
human needs. The result of this phase of authoritarianism is to put all values on one dead level, those
that are enduringly important, along with those that
are trivial, transitory, or totally irrelevant. If duty
is obedience to what is commanded, then Adam's eat-
ing of an apple is as bad as Cain's murder of Abel—
and conformity to ritual and its details is as good
as love and courage. The rivers of conscience are
poisoned at their source and the faculties of moral
discrimination and taste are vulgarized. The final
consequence to the child bred up in this ethic is that

if he loses his faith in the existence of the commander of duties, he will lose also his respect for the duties commanded. And when values which were defended on the ground of their descent from heaven are discovered to have had an earthly origin, their validity will seem impaired. For the fallacy of geneticism is twofold, and the primary error of accrediting an ideal by appeal to its claims of high descent begets the secondary error of discrediting it when its beginnings are discovered to be lowly. A conscience debauched by an inculcated respect for authority as such will, when deprived of that authority, have no longer the power to guide conduct.

I believe that it is not open to doubt that a large part of the immoralisms and confused egoisms of the day are due to the inevitable aftermath of a morality based on a divine power in whose existence faith has been lost. Those who sow the wind of theological authority are destined to reap the whirlwind of ethical confusion in the generations that follow.

Asceticism and Other-Worldliness.

WE have seen something of the way in which traditional religion in respect to its general method of authoritarianism has opposed itself to freedom of conscience and freedom of thought, and has to that extent paralyzed progress both in morals and in science. We have now to consider the second respect in which Christianity is alien to the modern temper, namely, in its defense of a life-negating conception of ethical values, according to which asceticism and

other-worldliness are substituted for the life-affirming ideals of self-realization and social betterment in
this world.

All morality begins with self-control. The impulse
of the moment is inhibited by the consciousness of
past pains and future pleasures, by sympathy for
the needs of other individuals, and by the restraints
of social custom. We save in order to spend and
forego the lesser for the greater satisfaction. Now
the ascetic is the *miser* of the spiritual life. For just
as the miser begins by saving as a means to spending,
and winds up by regarding saving as an end in itself,
so the ascetic begins by inhibiting some desires as a
means to gratifying others, and winds up by regarding inhibition as an end in itself. The world and the
flesh in which our lives are cast are treated as at war
with the spirit. The latter can thrive only at the
expense of the former. Abandonment of this world
and preoccupation with the world to come, mortifica-
tion of the flesh and exaltation of all that negates life
and the will to live, are made into ideals of righteousness, with the result that the religion thus tainted
by asceticism defends and enjoins in the name of
morality a complete inversion of moral values.

It is difficult to exaggerate the extent to which
these ascetic traditions are opposed to the modern
temper and the modern outlook. We live in an age
which, whatever its shortcomings in practice, is profoundly humanitarian in sentiment and imbued with
the faith that, in an evolving world, man can indefinitely improve the conditions of his earthly life.

To attack the fleshly appetites in place of harmoniz-
ing and perfecting them, and to make the prepara-
tion for heaven a substitute for good will on earth, is
to go directly counter to the highest and most significant ideals of our time.

To realize the strength of this phase of the anticlerical challenge to traditional religion it is not
necessary to apportion the responsibility for the in-
verted morality of asceticism among the various sects
who have variously contributed to it. Whether Paul
or Augustine was the most guilty, whether the concentrated asceticism imposed upon its clerics by Ca-
tholicism is worse than the wide and thin asceticism
of Protestant puritanism from which not only the
clergy but the laity must suffer, are questions into
which we need not go. Brought up as a Protestant I
find myself less repelled by the Catholic form of
asceticism than by the one I am used to. Foreign
slums have sometimes a picturesqueness that is lacking to those in one's own land; and I can contemplate
without indignation a community in which there is a
monastery on a hill wherein a group of ardent spirits
dedicate themselves freely and with single hearts to
repudiating the joys of what, no matter how errone-
ously, they believe to be a ruined world, while at the
village at the foot of the hill children may dance
around the Maypole unmolested and all laymen enjoy
an innocent pagan gaiety. When I turn from that
Latin community to the more familiar Anglo-Saxon
scene in which Puritanism expresses itself in Blue
Laws, Purity Leagues, Censorship, and Prohibition,

with all the allied forms of persecution, repression, and gloom, I can feel only disgust that the professed followers of Christ should so betray his teaching of the more abundant life.

Supernaturalism.

THE modern attacks upon the authoritarian method of traditional religion and upon its ascetic and other-worldly conception of ethics are closely related, at least in the minds of those who make them, to the objections to that metaphysics of supernaturalism which pervades not only the specific teachings of the Bible but its generic faith in a power that makes for good.

The stories of the Creation and the Fall and of the relations of the supernatural yet all too human Yahweh with his favorite People, contain just that blend of history and legend, fact and poetry, that is typical of an evolving tribal folklore. The Jews had more of the zeal for righteousness than the Greeks or any other nation, and their great contribution to the human race as a whole is their recognition that goodness is the highest form of good. The Old Testament is the immortal epic of the evolution of a deity, and the progressive moralization of Jehovah from the fantastic and vengeful demon of the earlier legends to the sublimely idealized God of justice and mercy of whom the Prophets sang, is the record—albeit written upon the sky—of the Jewish conscience in its progress from Moses to Jesus.

To trouble one's self with a serious refutation of

the literal and historic truth of the narrative is only less absurd than to accept it. While to attempt to save its authenticity by distorting its beautiful and simple cosmogony into a deliberately concocted allegory is an insult not only to our modern intelligence but to the sincerity and literary clarity of its writers. It would have been perfectly easy for the author of Genesis to have recounted the order of creation in such a way as to harmonize roughly with the evolutionary order as we now know it, had he possessed any inkling of that order. And if by "the evening and the morning were the first day" he had meant the end and beginning of a long period of time—a geological epoch—he could have simply said so, in perfect confidence that his hearers, no matter how mistaken their notions about the world, could have comprehended so plain a conception.

If we will for a moment imagine the Bible to have come suddenly to our attention today, unencumbered by a tradition of divine authority, and with no more sacredness than a newly discovered writing of ancient China or Egypt, we can see quite readily that it would occur to nobody who took the work merely on its merits either to accept it as scientifically and historically true, or to twist its statements into a far-fetched allegory of the truth.

When we turn from the Old Testament to the story of Christ that is contained in the New Testament, and also in the elaborations and supplementations of churchmen, we find a different and more extended supernaturalism. To the contribution of the Jews, preoccupied with their own history, there is added a Hellenic contribution in which scientific and metaphysical interests take precedence over the merely historical. A simple Jewish teacher with a mystic sense of his mission implores all men to dedicate their lives without reserve to the ideal of universal love and thereby gain eternal life. The teacher further gives assurance that whoever wills to have this infinite boon may gain it regardless of worldly status, strength, or learning—regardless even of past wickedness. His teaching puts the most high glory within the reach of the most lowly. This is, it seems to me, almost all that matters in the Christian ethics. To have discovered and proclaimed the way of absolute beauty and at the same time to have shown that it is free to all, and then to have lived gently and ardently and died terribly as a supreme exemplification of his own teaching, is enough for a son of God born of woman. For us to try to better the picture by ornamenting its frame with biological and psychological anomalies, such as a virgin birth and a miraculous absence of all sin and all ignorance, verges on the tawdry. For his immediate successors, however, it was understandable and pardonable enough, for they could see no better way of honoring their friend and celebrating the glory and solace of his message, than by following the well-worn path of mythological custom—first imputing to him a monopoly of all virtue and all wisdom, and then loading down his birth and life and death with physical signs and wonders.

It is not that the miraculous events in the narra-

tive are necessarily impossible, and it is even probable that some of the miracles of healing took place.
We could indeed go further, and on the assumption
of a cosmic life or soul which pervades all individual
lives, we could conceive of a miraculous fertilization
of the cell from which the body of Jesus grew on the
analogy of the life force of an organism directly
stimulating some one of the organs or cells. But no
such *tour de force* in speculative biology could really
add to the honor of him for whose benefit it was invoked. Moreover, if a physically divine genesis of
Jesus is desired, it could be had more simply by as-
suming his body to have had a natural bi-parental
origin and postulating a concomitant influx of the
world soul at the moment of conception. Yet even
this hypothesis is not requisite to an essential Christianity, for the fundamental basis of Christ's divinity
must rest upon the quality of his life rather than
upon anything physically peculiar in connection with
its origin. If his life had started at the ordinary human level and he had made it into what it was, he
would have been a no less significant figure. To earn
divinity with the handicap of a complete humanity
is at least as inspiring as to have inherited it as an
initial gift.

If we turn from these points of Christian super-
naturalistic history to the more properly metaphysical doctrine of the Trinity, we find ourselves on very
different ground. The origin and guidance of the
world is postulated as spiritual, that is, as intelligent
and benign. The divine being has three aspects or

functions which, without prejudice to its substantial unity, are to be conceived as "persons." First, there is God the Father, absolute and ultimate source of all things, both abstract and concrete, a mystic blend of the Neo-Platonic One, and Jehovah, creator of the world. Second, there is God the Son, who, like the Father, has both an abstract and a concrete reality. As abstract he is the Logos, or totality of all essences logically derivable from the Father, but integrated and morally harmonized into an archetypal personality, the Christ. As concrete, the divine personality is exemplified in space and time as the man Jesus, by whose suffering and death the Creator shares the woes of his creatures and so redeems them. Third, there is God in his aspect of immanent sustainer, inspirer, and comforter of all beings—the Holy Ghost.

Whatever one may think of the truth of this trinitarian metaphysics, it was an amazing achievement of the creative imagination. It fused Jewish history, natural and supernatural, with a characteristically Hellenistic metaphysics, closely resembling Neo-Platonism. But the new system was far from being merely an eclectic composite of two heterogeneous traditions. For the life and death and teachings of Jesus which constituted the heart of the new doctrine, differentiated it from its borrowed components and conferred upon it a superiority to each of them. The notion of a God loving the world enough to suffer and die for it put the whole conception of Divinity in a new light. The irresponsible and often cruel Jehovah was himself in a very real sense redeemed by his

identification with Christ. And with respect to the
Greek factor the superiority of the new system was
equally well marked. For the ideal of human perfection, as definable in terms of the divine personality
of Christ, gave emphasis to the ultimate and irreplaceable validity of the category of person, in contrast to the tendency to pantheistic impersonalism
which was latent in the Neo-Platonic metaphysics.
And in the second place, the rôle of the man Jesus as
an actual participant in earthly history, a suffering
and best loved friend, gave the Christian religion a
concrete hold upon the lives of its members that no
mere system of abstract philosophy could possibly
exert.

There is today a widespread and increasing belief
that the minimum essentials of Christian supernaturalism which I have just attempted to present in outline, have been rendered antiquated, false, and absurd
by our modern knowledge. Let us consider the arguments in support of this anti-Christian belief.

The world as we know it today differs from the
world as known in the early centuries in the three following respects:

1. The size of the world in space and its duration
in time have been extended beyond all resemblance to
the dimensions accepted by the Church Fathers. The
Copernican revolution followed by the ideas of as-
tronomical, geological, and biological evolution, combined to present us with a universe that up to a few
years ago appeared to be infinite both in space and
in time. And even though the recent Einsteinian views

of a finite space based upon Relativity, and of a finite time or history based upon the new emphasis on the increase of entropy and the transformation of matter into radiation, advocated by Jeans and Eddington, be accepted, the Neo-Ptolemaic and Neo-Mosaic universe of the twentieth century is still enormously greater in size and duration than the early Christian world.

Yet after all, mere bigness itself is not incompatible with the theistic hypothesis. Any deity that could pervade the ancient world with a diameter of perhaps 10^{10} miles and a duration of several thousand years, could about equally well inhabit our present world with its diameter of 10^{20} miles and its duration of a quadrillion or so of years. And even if we should have to undo the counter-revolution of Einstein and Eddington and return to the spacious Copernican universe of the nineteenth century, I do not see why Giordano Bruno's postulate of an infinite spirit pervading an infinite body is not as plausible now as when it was first uttered. But though the spatio-temporal expansions of modern astronomic and evolutionary science do not render impossible the core of Christian metaphysics, they do quite definitely destroy such concomitants as the cosmogony and chronology of the Bible and its cosmographic conceptions of Heaven and Hell. These latter doctrines are, however, so repugnant to the ethical outlook of today that their incompatibility with history and physics hardly needs mention.

2. The aspect of modern knowledge that counts

much more seriously against Christian supernaturalism than the mere enlargement of the universe is the
change from the anthropocentric to the cosmo-centric
conception of man's place in that world. It is not the
largeness and duration of nature, but the indifference
of her structure and processes to us and our planet
that really matter. Our species is one of many that
have evolved from the lowest specks of life. Our earth
is one of many similar satellites of a star which is an
insignificant member of a galaxy which is itself but
one of many galaxies. Man's physical form and his
physical dwelling place are no longer unique. The
heavens do not revolve around us, the earth was not
prepared for us any more than for our near cousins
the apes or our distant cousins the fleas, or our still
more remote relatives of the vegetable kingdom. The
better we understand the laws of nature the more
indifferent to our weal and woe do they appear. In
the light of all this there are many who feel that the
assumption of any sort of personal god with a human-
like love for human animals is immeasurably absurd,
and explainable only as a relic of primitive ignorance
and fear.

Then, too, the seemingly lifeless and valueless portion of nature is enormously greater than the living
part. And even if we set this down to our ignorance,
and consider only the living part, we find by far the
greater part of that to be either valueless or possessed
of negative value. Evolution presents a spectacle in
which for every success there are a thousand failures,
and for every continuing life a thousand deaths. Life

subsists upon life and we have reached and maintain our present modest estate at the cost of uncountable failures and agonies on the part of our victims. To believe that a personal spirit, with the resources of omniscience and omnipotence, planned such a world, is to attribute to him an amount of blundering and cruelty that would make the meanest of men seem saintly by contrast. It resembles the belief in the literal truth of the Bible, in being a theory that would occur to no mind however simple without the aid of a strong subconscious hope or fear.

It is of course true that the indifference of the world to the values of living beings is no recent discovery. But modern science, though it has not originated it, has nevertheless given to it a new and terrible emphasis. It is not merely that the universe is so large and we so small; it is the teeth and claws with which nature is red, and her terrible unconcern for the children which she so prodigally creates that is of real significance.

In closing our discussion of the second indictment of the supernaturalism of traditional religion, we may remark that it is directed mainly against the hypothesis of a God who is omnipotent. The extent to which it would apply against the existence of another sort of deity we shall consider in the last chapter.

3. The third challenge to religious supernaturalism is based on the materialistic or mechanistic conception of mind and life. The tenor of the argument has not changed much since the days of Hobbes

and Spinoza, or even of Lucretius and Democritus, though during the last century many new domains of nature have yielded to mechanism's power to predict and control and, in a sense, to explain the course of events. The argument can be stated in two parts. First, in one region after another in which effects once seemed to necessitate internal and purposeful causes, of a conscious if not supernatural character, there have been found natural causes of an external quantitative and unpurposive kind which seem to be adequate. And the plausible inference is advanced that if we knew more of the facts of nature, we should be able to explain all by the methods which have already explained so much. The second part of the argument applies not to the cosmos generally, but to the conscious individual. It can be summarized in the following premise and conclusion:

Mind and its processes vary concomitantly with matter and its processes, therefore mind is a function of matter dependent upon its mechanistic laws and inseparable from its admittedly perishable aggregates.

There are probably more people today than ever before who accept these arguments as valid, and as precluding the religious belief in a mind-like and purposeful power in the world. With the main issue involved in these mechanistic attacks upon supernaturalism, I shall attempt to deal in the concluding chapter. I will merely remark in passing that the parts of nature that have been most successfully annexed to the domain of the materialistic, have been either inorganic processes, or else very secondary aspects of organic processes. Nor can I see that the evidence of modern science takes us much further toward the reduction of mind and its purposes to an ineffective and adjectival accompaniment of blindly moving particles in our bodies, than did the philosophy of an earlier day. We know very many more of the correlations and very many more of the details of the body's structure than were known in ancient times. For example, we know that it is the brain with its glands, rather than the heart, liver, or spleen, that is directly correlated with the cognitive and affective states of consciousness. For the vaguely conceived animal spirits of the Cartesians flowing through little pipes to the pineal gland and out again, we substitute the elaborate network of afferent and efferent nerve tracts conveying forms of energy to and from the cerebral cortex. For the weird conceptions of embryonic development current of old, we have knowledge of the detailed series of structures from the heredity-bearing genes through the blastula, gastrula, and subsequent phases of gestation. But I do not see that, with all this, we are much nearer than our ancestors to understanding how the organism as a whole is to be explained for what it is in terms of the clear and simple laws that are applicable to the particles that compose it.

Conclusion.

AND now to conclude: We essayed first to give a definition of religion that should avoid not only the crude absurdities of primitive superstition, but also the sophisticated truisms of the various naturalisms and humanisms of the present day. Nobody denies that there is some sort of mysterious background for the detailed phenomena of nature, and nobody denies that an improved or perfected humanity is worth striving for. If the word God is to mean merely one or the other of these things, and if religion is to mean merely a more or less impassioned recognition of these truisms, accompanied, perhaps, with sufficient remnants of ancient ritual to make possible the use of the temples and their endowments, the whole matter is simply not worth discussion.

If, however, religion is taken to mean the faith, theoretical, practical, and emotional, in something in nature that is making for the values that we cherish, then religion in that sense is at least important. It may be as false and as bad as the militant atheists of the Soviet Union believe. Or it may be as true and essential to human good as the Christian Fundamentalists, Catholic or Protestant, hold it to be. It is at any rate a thing to discuss.

Taking religion in this sense, we attempted a rapid survey of the principal arguments that at the present time especially are urged against the doctrines of traditional Christianity. We discussed the authoritarianism of its general methodology, the asceticism and other-worldliness of its ethics, and the supernaturalism of its metaphysics. As regards the methodological and ethical indictments we were in accord with the critics and their destructive conclusions; but with the attacks on supernaturalism we were in only partial agreement. Our task in the chapters that follow is the more difficult one of outlining a religious ethics and metaphysics that will be less open to the kind of objections that have here been considered.

II

A SANCTIONLESS MORALITY

ALL bodies are both agents and patients. They initiate changes and suffer them. Living bodies differ from others in that their agency exceeds their patience. They give to their environment more alteration than they receive from it.

The power of a non-living body to preserve and impose its form is proportionate to its energy. In a living body the power to preserve and impose its form is out of all proportion to its energy. A little yeast will leaven much dough. A group of men can change a continent.

Whence comes this prepotency of a living organism in every encounter with the not-self? We can give at least a provisional answer. The living being can inform its present environment because it has been informed by its past environments. Retaining traces of these past encounters it accumulates a wealth of forms, and is thereby differentiated from those dead things which spend all they receive and save nothing. Every body *has* its history but a living body *is* its history. Its past is not only past but also present and operative. It is then because the organism preserves its past history that it possesses potentialities for determining its future history.

The movements of a body possessed of potentialities vary primarily with its inner states and only secondarily with its outer circumstances. If its potentialities change, its behavior will vary though the environment remains the same. While conversely if external circumstances change, the potentiality will manifest its steadfast influence in bringing the organism, though by devious routes, to the same original goal.

The presence of bodies possessed of this vital prepotency confers a new and relativistic status upon the objects composing their environment. For those objects, in addition to being what they are intrinsically and absolutely, will now be divided with respect to each organism into those that fulfil directly or indirectly the potentialities of that organism and those that thwart or counteract them. This new status which objects acquire relatively to organisms is the status of *value*.

It is obvious that if there were no prepotencies or potentialities, there would be no such thing as objects of value in the sense in which I shall use the term "value." It is equally true, though not so obvious, that if the prepotency of a body were infinite or absolute, its potentialities would be actualized irrespective of any objects, and so again nothing external to it could possess value. An object has value to the extent that it can fulfil a potentiality.

Now potentiality is a word that is greatly in disfavor with present-day philosophers, and I should like to mitigate objection to its use by making its meaning more specific as applied to life systems. When a mass is removed from the center of gravity of its system, it is given a potentiality of returning to that center. When a body is compressed like a

spring or like a ball thrown against a wall, it receives
a potentiality. But these potentialities, which are
called potential energy of position and potential energy of elasticity, are each of them potentialities of
mere motion. And for their actualization they demand only the release from the supporting or com-
pressing force. The specific potentialities of protoplasm are potentialities of form, or structure, or
pattern, rather than of mere motion; and they mainly
require for their actualization not the subtraction of
a matter that hinders but the addition of a matter
that helps. For example, digested food particles are
brought by the blood to the cell units of lung or
liver. By means of the complex pattern of forces
characterizing the tissue in question, the incoming
matter is rearranged to conform to the structure of
the cell. This is assimilation or anabolism, the fundamental property of life. It is a transfer, or rather an
imposition (analogous to electrostatic or magnetic
induction), of a complex form of organization, from
matter that had it and retains it, to matter that did
not have it before but now acquires it. The hungry
cell is satisfied. Its stock of matter and energy has
been added to, its form is preserved, its potentiality
fulfilled. But its potentiality was fulfilled by the addition of new material. It has grown or increased at
the expense of the food that composed its environment. Just as the potentiality of an atomic nucleus
expressed in the positive electric field surrounding
it is actualized or satisfied by its growth into a full
or non-ionized atom by the capture of the negative

electrons that complement it, so the living and growing cell fulfils its potentialities by assimilation of external but complementary substances. Of course there
is the opposite process of katabolism, in which energy
is spent in action, tissue depleted, waste accumulated,
and death attained. But I cannot but feel that it is
the anabolic phase of metabolism in which potentialities are actualized by that selective increase of substance which we call growth, including its climactic
episode of reproduction, that differentiates living
from non-living matter.

Now when we pass from vegetative life or mere life
through animal to man, and consider not man's body
but his mind, we find again a typical vital system—
an accumulation of traces of past encounters with
the environment and a resulting prepotency over it,
comprised of potentialities. This secondary organism
of mind differs from the primary organism that is
its matrix in that it is constituted of sensory forms
instead of material substances. The energy taken
into the organism with food and air is embodied in
material particles. The stimuli that come to the brain
over the nerves are forms of energy merely. At the
synapses or points of re-direction they pass from the
kinetic to the potential phase and are experienced as
sensations. And after all, or almost all, has been
changed back into motion and conveyed out over the
efferent nerves, their traces or forms are left in the
brain and constitute the steadily growing system of
memories. The potentialities of this psychic organism
are experienced as desires or as impulses according to

whether they are or are not accompanied by images of their objects. A psychic potentiality requires for its actualization the attainment of an object, just as much as the potentiality of a bodily cell requires for its object the matter that it will assimilate. But in the case of the mind, actualization of its potentialities consists in the attainment not of material particles but of experiences such as the smell of food, the sight of a friend, or the solution of a problem. These experiences are psychic food. They are assimilated or anabolized and added as increments to the substance of the self. Any object that will fulfil one of these potentialities, along with whatever is instrumental to such fulfilment, *has value* or *is a value* in the literal or experiential sense. When a desired object is being attained normally and, as it were, at a uniform rate, the feeling-tone of our experience is bare contentment; but when the process is facilitated or accelerated, pleasure is felt; when it is thwarted or retarded, unpleasantness is felt. The realization that a value has actually been attained is happiness; that it has actually been frustrated is grief.

This biological introduction to ethical problems may seem irrelevant. I have given it for two closely related reasons: First, because I believe that the resemblance of the mind and its ideational activities to the body and its physical life is more than a mere illustrative analogy. The mind is itself an organism —an organism within an organism. It is composed of sensory forms of energy as truly as is its matrix composed of material or embodied forms of energy.

And to understand what mind is it is necessary to understand its literally vital nature. Secondly and more specifically: The attainment of value must be interpreted as an increment of psychic substance. It constitutes an actual growth of one's very being. So while I can agree with the utilitarians that whatever satisfies desire or gives pleasure is a value, or with Professor R. B. Perry's definition of value as "any object of any interest," yet I feel that such conceptions, while true as far as they go, possess a certain thinness. They are too formal and too restrictedly psychological; they cry out for a concrete ontological filling that will integrate the thing called value with the nature of the existence which it should qualify, and not leave it floating mysteriously and relegated exclusively to a realm of its own. My conception of the ideal as increment of the real, the *ought* as the dynamic and growing aspect of the *is*, in short, of value as the actualization of potentiality, seems to me to supplement the too subjective and psychologistic tradition of hedonism with an objective and quasi-material factor in which that tradition is lacking. I agree with the ethical relativism of the utilitarian, and I admit that value is any object of any interest. But I want to be told what an interest is, and to get some light on how and why such a thing as interest or desire comes to be, and to be itself an effective component of the very world which it seeks to transform. The biological approach to ethics which I have essayed does not answer perfectly these questions but it does answer them to some extent.

The Sentiment of Approval.

In any ethical discussion the concept next in importance to value itself, and in a certain sense even more fundamental, is that which we call "approval." When there are various theories of value contending for acceptance, the bar before which they must be brought for final judgment, is the sentiment of *approval*. Which is the valid ethical theory—the Utilitarianism which with additions I have accepted, or Egoism, or Rigorism, or some type of Religious Authoritarianism? How can we answer such a question except by an overt and shameless *petitio principii* in favor of one of the partisans? If I, as a utilitarian, wished to persuade a non-utilitarian of the truth of my ethics, I should make small headway if I took for granted what he denied. All that any ethical theorist can do is to set forth his conceptions and submit them to that sentiment of approval which all moralists have in common, and trust that the new light in which he has exhibited his own theory will make it appeal to his opponent as worthy of approval.

Approval is valuation of the second order; it is an evaluation of values. How is this possible, and how are we to understand it? There are two ways in which a sensory object can conform to our liking and actualize our potentialities; first, by the relation of its material existence to our material existence; second, by the relation of its form to the forms in us, irrespective of the bearing of its existence upon our existence. In the first case the value is merely hedonic;

in the second case it is aesthetic. Beauty is not the externalization of *any* pleasure, but of such pleasure only as comes from the essence of an object rather than from its causal relation to our practical needs. We can check the truths of this Kantian conception of aesthetic value on the objective side by realizing that if a thing appreciated as beautiful were suddenly discovered to be a pure hallucination with no existence of its own in external nature, its beauty would not be in any sense diminished by the discovery. We can also check the truth of the theory from the subjective side by realizing that the aesthetic significance of a spectacle would be impaired or destroyed if it were made to depend upon our practical and existential participation in it. Every picture must in some sense have a frame that will isolate its episodes from the world in which the observer stands and with reference to which his existence is oriented. The frame on which a drama depends for its beauty is the stage which insulates the actors and their deeds from the spectator and his friends. This separation of the observer and his world from the world that is aesthetically observed is the basis of Kant's conception of disinterested pleasure, and equally of what Mr. Bullough has called "psychic distance." Psychic distance is the distance across the abyss separating the universe of sensory contemplation from the universe of action. For practical intercourse the abyss is properly impassable. Only aesthetic experience achieves the miracle and, spanning the chasm between the spirit of the beholder and the beauty that is beheld, joins them in a union that is at once Platonic and at the same time more perfect and intimate than any to be found in sensory experience, save one.

Now the valuing evidenced in approval is to mere valuing or desire as the aesthetic is to the merely hedonic. It is in short a valuation that is disinterested, and by that token authenticated. Trembling with terror, I yet give my approval to courage. Torn with jealousy and hatred, I see only too well that it is magnanimity and charity that are good. For them my spirit pathetically yearns and them it categorically approves at the very moment that my flesh, the existential me, winces and turns away. This sentiment of approval is conscience. It is a faculty of disinterested interest, the bar of judgment before which must come all proposals, both of moral practice and of ethical theory.

What is the nature, and, more specifically, what is the origin of this conscience, this strange body of impersonal evaluations that constitutes the moral sense of every person?

The Threefold Structure of Conscience.

THE human animal is selfish, sympathetic, and suggestible. Like other animals he retains and stores up traces of past happenings, and his reaction to an environing object at any moment is determined partly by the object's relation to him as he actually is at the moment, and partly by its relation to the history within him, and to the potentialities comprising that history. Along with the traces of past sensations which sometimes recur of themselves as images, and which at all times clothe the later sensations with meaning and so transform them into perceptions, there are also the traces of the motor tendencies, the likes and dislikes associated with these sensations. It is these attractions and repulsions that make up the system of controls that we call conscience. Conscience is present in a limited form in the lower animals. A dog seizes a piece of meat and is whipped for it. The next day the impulse to do the same thing is inhibited by the memory of the pain attendant on it in the past. (*Self-interest.*) Or, again, the same dog will forego yielding to a hunger impulse in order to feed her puppies. (*Sympathy.*) Or, again, the barking and running of her fellow canines, or the well-known voice of her master, may serve to control more direct impulses to gratify the need of her own organism. (*Suggestibility.*) The validity of such illustrations of animal conscience is not dependent upon any illegitimate or questionable reconstruction of the brute consciousness in terms of our own. It is sufficient to take the matter objectively and behavioristically, and to observe that an animal acts *as if* the simpler and more immediate tendencies were guided, controlled, and, at times, prevented by a larger but less immediate system, based upon imitation and suggestion, upon sympathy, and upon memory of past pains and pleasures.

On the human level of behavior we can discover at first hand in ourselves the presence and more or less effective operation of the same threefold system. And it is undoubtedly infinitely more extensive in each of its three aspects than in the brute. In the first place, our self-interest may extend beyond the just impending act to contingencies years in advance, even to our posthumous and eternal future. In the second place, our sympathies, instead of being restricted to the parental interest in which they probably originated, extend to whole families, tribes, and nations, even to other species, and to the yet unborn. In the third place, our suggestibility or imitativeness embraces all tendencies to do what is commanded, proposed, or even expected by others, and to conform ourselves not merely to what we see and hear, as in modes of dress and speech, but to the actions, beliefs, and sentiments of others, even of those we may despise, or of those of whose existence we may be in doubt. Our own past thoughts and actions are included among the things we imitate, and constitute our conformity to habit, which is the narrowest and most stubborn of all the orthodoxies.

The still small voice of conscience, the curiously stern and impersonal, yet curiously internal judgment of moral approval or disapproval, brought to bear upon any proposal, practical or theoretical, is the crystallization of that whole enormous system of controls which constitutes our larger self. Conscience is indeed the call of the larger and higher, but fainter, self, with its triple set of potentialities, to the narrow but sensuously vivid and concrete self of the here and now. It is to action what intelligence is to apprehension and serves as the conative analogue of the cognitive apperception mass. And as the apperception mass, or body of acquired meanings, functions to correct the distorted perspective of mere sensory impressions, so conscience functions to correct the equally distorted perspective of mere sensuous impulse. For it is conscience that warns us that "another man's blood is as red as our own," his joys and sorrows as poignant and real as ours, and that the greater good of tomorrow, pale as it may appear, is really more important than the lesser good of the moment, with all its warm and vivid appeal.

Now if we allow ourselves to be too much impressed with the quantitative extent, vast though it is, of the human as compared with the animal conscience, we shall miss the most important attribute of man, the attribute that constitutes him not merely a separate species, but a kingdom distinct from all other earthly creatures. In the long course of evolution there came a time when the cognitive and conative traces of past experience acquired sufficient strength to dominate the sensory structures from which they grew, and to attain a kind of autonomy. Memories ceased to be merely the adjectives of sensation and the instruments of practical guidance. Their appearances in consciousness ceased to be determined exclusively by the practical exigencies of the situation. Free images arising from the past were able to maintain themselves, even under the fierce light of sensations. The brute learned to dream, while still awake, of things absent and remote in space and time. The waking dreams and the absent-mindedness marked the emergence of a higher level of life, that of human life. The body and the whole material world now became, at least potentially and intermittently, the servant of mind rather than its master. Mind thus emancipated and autonomous is spirit, and spirit ranges where it will, far beyond the here and now, and even beyond the space and time to which existence is confined. Imagination has become creative, intelligence has become reason, animal training has become deliberate morality, and man, entering his new kingdom of abstract ideas and ideal values, makes far-flung plans for subduing and informing with spirit the very material nature on which his existence depends. And coeval with this evolution of rational being, comes the evolution of cries into speech. The new verbal symbols constitute a sensory body for the delicate and precarious creations of spirit. For language is the savior of thought, and without it our ideas and ideals would lapse back and be lost in the flux of sensations from which they emerged. It is by means of words that the conceptions enshrined in them can be organized as a culture, and transmitted, enduring and growing, from generation to generation.

It is good that man's conscience comprises the three groups of higher potentialities that we have designated as self-interest, sympathy, and suggestibility. But it is not good that the third factor, suggestibility, should be the most important, for it alone is purely provisional, secondary, and instrumental to the other two. Yet the feeling that, above all else, we ought to do what we have been told to do, is by

far the strongest of our moral controls. Obedience
to authority and conformity to custom are of neces-
sity the first things in a child's education, but an
ethics that continues to interpret value in terms of
obedience and conformity is an ethics that is childish.
The human race as a whole cannot attain rationality
and maturity until it puts away the attitudes suited
to the first prerational years of its individual members. How deeply our ethics is tainted with this prolongation of infancy is shown by the etymology of
ethical terms. Not only the words *ethics* and *morals*
themselves (signifying customs), but such words as
law and *commandment* are felt to be appropriate
names for duty. We need only a momentary scrutiny
of what the words actually imply to perceive their
irrelevance and absurdity. For when a custom is once
clearly recognized as bad, the feeling of obligation to
conform to it vanishes. It is only when the *mores* are
themselves moral that they can claim our respect.
We are similarly handicapped in our discussion by
having to use misnomers in the case of commandment
and law. If we were convinced that an evil power had
given us ten commandments and had laid down a law
for us to obey, we should feel it our moral duty to
disobey such laws and commandments; and what
obedience we rendered would be due to craven fear
and against our conscience. In short, there is nothing
that is in any way good about a custom as such, a
law as such, a commandment as such. Whatever
goodness they may claim is due exclusively to such
prospects as they may directly or indirectly offer

of satisfying a need or actualizing a potentiality, and thus conferring upon some life system, one's own or another's, that increase of psychic being which alone is the essence of value. It is remarkable that, while everybody admits this when his attention is called to it, hardly anybody recognizes it *until* his attention is called to it. The purpose of Ethics is to rationalize Morals, and the difficulty of that enterprise is mainly due to the non-rational element in conscience resulting from that prolongation of infancy to which we have referred. Because of the mind's sensitiveness to suggestion, conscience becomes filled with feelings of obligation to perform certain acts and refrain from certain others, for no reason at all except that they were originally suggested or commanded. To make the matter worse, the cogency of these feelings often varies inversely with their reasonableness. Civilized adults, as well as savages and children, feel most strongly about those duties for which they can find no justification. A rule of moral action for which there is no reason in fact, or even in fancy, will be called a *taboo* by a person who does not himself feel it. But if the critic is in his turn the victim of feelings of reasonless obligation, he will call them not "taboos" but "categorical imperatives." To replace these causeless or categorical imperatives by hypothetical imperatives, where the feeling of what is right is justified by the knowledge that what is good will ensue, is the primary task for ethical theory and also the prerequisite for a sound and progressive morality.

That we should feel an obligation to act without reason is the first paradox of which a philosophy of value must take account. The second paradox consists in the truth that as long as we have such feelings of duty, it is our duty to follow them. The recognition of the *de facto* conscience must not wait upon its *de jure* authentication, desirable though that may be, for, in the case of duty, *esse est percipi*. It is here that the traditional utilitarians have been wrong and the intuitionists and rigorists have been right. And, stranger still, the unsoundness of the utilitarian tradition on this point is demonstrable from premises that are themselves ultimately and properly utilitarian. For the respect in which man differs utterly from his animal ancestors is in his attainment of *spirit;* and spirit, as we have seen, is that which mind becomes when emancipated from exclusive service of the body. It is an infinite and self-perpetuating system of potentialities, and confers upon its possessor an extra dimension of substance, with the result that, as the smallest increment of a volume is incommensurably greater than the largest increment of a mere surface or plane, so are the increments of spirit incommensurably greater than those of sense. This is why it is better to be good than to be wise, better to actualize a mistaken, and even a mischievous, ideal, if honestly believed in, than to do what may turn out to be objectively good at the price of disloyalty to one's own conscience. This is why we give unconditional respect to the man who, from moral obligation, would do that which we ourselves are morally obligated to prevent. We can restrain and even punish him for his error, and at the same time honor him for his intrinsic nobility in living according to his light. The intuitionists were right in their conclusion that no amount of happiness in pigs can equal the happiness of a Socrates, but neither they nor Mill himself were right in inferring that the incommensurability of the two happinesses implied a difference with respect to some quality other than happiness itself. It is not a mysterious quality other than satisfactoriness that makes the satisfactions essential to virtue incommensurable with those of sense. If that were so the true good would consist in that mysterious quality, and rationality in ethics would be rendered impossible. Spirit and its potentialities derive their incommensurable dignity, not from an alien and absolute quality, but from the infinity of quantity by which their dimension exceeds the lesser dimension of bodily needs. Not merely in intensity and duration but in volume and depth do values differ from one another. Maximum of satisfaction, or life-fulfilment, is the one and only moral absolute, the *summum bonum*. The rightness of an action or of a rule of action is proportionate to the extent to which it serves as a means to that end. The *de facto* conscience of a man is the primary means to that end and should be unconditional, but the education of that conscience, the clarification of moral feeling by ethical insight, is also a means to the supreme goal. And it is our contention that the clarification of conscience can come only through cleansing and purging it of all taboos, all unreasoned devotions, all categorical imperatives which, when followed, bring salvation to the individual soul but retard the progress of the world. Interest in perfecting one's life and the lives of others by quickening and intensifying existing potentialities, extending their number and scope, organizing them so that their conflicts will be harmonized, and then mobilizing all the energies of will and intellect to bring them to actuality, and thus add cubits to the stature of our being, that, as I see it, is the whole field of duty.

If the views just expressed are correct it will be apparent that the old question as to whether an individual can have a duty to himself will be quickly answered in the affirmative. My duty is to seek the greater rather than the lesser life. Conscience is the call of the potentially larger to the potentially smaller self. When the neighbors are present and I can help to realize potentialities in them it will be my duty so to serve them. But when the opportunity to enhance life is restricted to one person, namely myself, it is none the less my duty to fulfil a maximum of the potentialities offered. The notion that morality is exclusively social and that unless a man has neighbors making judgments and demands upon him all courses of action are morally indifferent to him—this seems to me absurd. Robinson Crusoe, for example, had the option of curling up and dying or of carrying on as he did and making the most of the life that was available. The presence of other people could have given him new duties but they would in no sense have been needed to validate his original duty to make his own life as abundant and as beautiful as possible.

Egoism and Altruism.

WHAT is the bearing of the theory that we have outlined upon the problem of egoism and altruism?

On the side of egoism it can be claimed that all actions must in some sense be of interest to the agent performing them; for otherwise they would be irrelevant and incapable of exerting any claim upon him. And how can a proposed action be of interest to an individual unless it promises to satisfy that interest? From which it would seem to follow that every deed must be done to satisfy the ego who performs it.

On the side of altruism it may be said that goodness and beauty are what they are wherever they are, and that to hold that all of my really reasonable actions must be directed to satisfying my own ego, is tantamount to holding that the whole universe of value is located in my ego, a doctrine of ethical solipsism at least as absurd as the better known metaphysical solipsism. For to recognize an action possible for me as good is identical with feeling the obligation to perform it. Consequently, to restrict the entire field of my duty to myself is to restrict to the limited confines of my own soul the entire field of what I can recognize as good. But how preposterous it would be for a person to believe that his own joys were the only real joys in the universe, or that the

sorrows of other men were not as genuinely sorrowful
as his own!

The way out of this *impasse*, and the consequent
reconciliation of the element of psychological validity
in egoism with the objective validity of an altruistic
or universalistic recognition of good as good, wherever or in whomsoever it is found, lies in the realization that (as the late Professor Herbert Lord used to
phrase it) the ego is itself an indeterminate affair.
As a thoroughly consistent egoist, I have to consider
not only what will most satisfy my ego as it now is,
but also what kind of ego it would most satisfy me
to be. The quantity of an ego's satisfaction is like
the quantity of material motion. The latter depends
not merely on the intensity of the velocity, but also
upon the size or mass of the body that is moving. So
the quantity of an ego's satisfaction depends not only
on the intensity of the satisfaction, but also upon the
size of the ego that is being satisfied. The ego of a
hero or saint who includes in his own interests the
interests of others is just that much more of an ego.
And the satisfaction of that large and sympathetic
self (the "conjunct self," as Professor Palmer has
termed it), is incomparably more in total magnitude
than the pleasures (equal or even greater in intensity) of some poor little self whose range of interests
is restricted to the values occurring within his own
skin. We may illustrate our conception of satisfaction as a magnitude determined by two variables, the
intensity of the feeling and the volume or size of the
ego that feels it, by imagining ourselves delegated to

convert some prosperous scoundrel who justified his
sins by appealing to the ethics of egoism. To our
prayers that he alter his mode of living, at least to
the extent of ceasing to make others miserable, he
will reply that his life satisfies him better than any
other, that his lack of sympathy for the suffering he
causes is really one of his best assets, for it permits
him to enjoy himself to the full, untroubled by qualms
of pity. Our claim that he ought to act differently for
the sake of others, simply doesn't interest him. He
isn't interested in others; he happens to be interested
only in himself. We may then try two ancient lines of
appeal, the one external,—social, or natural, or supernatural—the other internal and psychological.
We remind him of the powers of the state and of
society to punish and reward. He will answer that of
course he recognizes those powers and that he will
not attempt to do more than he can safely get away
with, but he has found that that is considerable. Regarding nature and the extent to which breaches of
so-called natural laws bring pain and ill health, he
will again be on his guard and take such precautions
as prudence dictates. But society not always, and
nature never, metes out punishment for murder or
theft as such, but only for certain avoidable and non-
ethical concomitants of those crimes. Finally we appeal to the supernatural, to God. To which our egoist
will probably reply that to judge by the extent to
which the wicked prosper, there either is no God or,
if there is, then that God, for reasons best known to
himself, leaves the just and the unjust to go their

own ways. In any event, the egoist prefers the high probability of earthly pleasures to the remote and shadowy values of some other world.

We now take the other line of appeal. We tell him that virtue is its own reward, that the true sage would be happy even on the rack, and that an egoist who prefers purely selfish gratification to the pleasure of conscientious self-approval is choosing the lesser pleasure and cheating himself. The answer to this argument will probably be both prompt and contemptuous. Like others he has had moments when his selfish philosophy was not operating and when he followed his sense of duty. He has therefore experienced the pleasures of conscience, such as they are, but he finds them pale and thin as compared with other pleasures that he knows of. As to the holy men who are alleged to derive pleasure in doing the right even under torture, he begs leave to doubt their existence and, in any event, he is himself not so constituted. Perhaps he concludes his answer with the sneer that the fantastic psychology that we have invoked for his benefit is, if anything, more foolish and more hypocritical than the bogeys of theology on which our earlier exhortations were based. For while the belief in a hell and heaven is only highly improbable, the nonsense about the great ecstasy attendant upon the doing of duty is demonstrably false.

Up to this point the egoist has, it seems to me, all the best of the discussion, as conducted on these ancient lines. But before leaving him to stew in his sin, there is a third way that we may take. It is the way that proceeds from our theory that the greatness of a satisfaction depends not merely upon its intensity as felt, but also, and more importantly, upon the breadth and depth of the ego to which the satisfaction pertains. Let us then ask of our opponent whether he would not prefer to have his own friend or his own child constituted with a will to follow a broad and heroic, rather than a narrow and selfish, plan of life. Now, if he is not merely a scoundrel, but also an intelligent person and capable of honesty of judgment, at least in his philosophic moments, I think that to this question he will reply in the affirmative; and if we then press him further and inquire whether, as far as he himself is concerned, he would not have preferred that nature had cast him for the heroic rôle that he admires in others rather than for the little egoistic rôle that he finds himself to be enacting, I think that again he would say "Yes." Is there indeed anyone who would not prefer (if it were only possible) to be the great self, broadened by sympathy to include the interests of others and to realize that he had done the things that he would admire in others (quite apart from any reward, and no matter at what sacrifice) than to be what he is— a small and narrow ego, lacking interests in anything beyond himself? But our opponent will doubtless supplement these concessions with the statement that while it would assuredly give him immeasurable satisfaction to be other and finer than he is, yet, after all, we are what we are, and he, being what he is, actually prefers his own admittedly ignoble career of self-aggrandizement to the alternatives to which we have exhorted him.

This brings us to a new issue. Is it really necessary for any man to be what he is, and to like the things that he does like? Rather is it not always possible for us to make ourselves over and to change our existing nature and its desires?

Determinism and Free Will.

A MERE thing is mainly determined to behave as it does by its spatial or external relations to other things. To be sure, even here it is not the external relations alone, but the nature of the thing in those relations. The heavy stone behaves differently from the lighter one, the cube from the sphere, carbon from oxygen, even when the external factors are constant. But the internal nature of a lifeless body is itself reducible to external relations between its particles, and at the limit of such reductive analysis the final particles would be nothing but *foci* of spatial relations. This is the ideal of mechanism, and it is attained with successively higher degrees of approximation by the successive divisions and subdivisions of the bodies concerned. Atomism is the handmaid of mechanism, the potent methodological instrument by means of which occult internal self-determination is externalized away, and replaced by a publicly observable and mathematically calculable network of determinations *ab extra*.

Living bodies resist this spatialization of their determinants and compel us to recognize that not space only or mainly, but time, is their primary *milieu*. A living being, and, *a fortiori*, a conscious and rationally conscious living being, acts in conformity to its history. Its past is present and operative in it, and, as we have seen, its potentialities for the future are correlates of its traces of the past. This is part of what we mean when we say that persons are free rather than fated. A man is self-determined; his acts flow from his character; he can do what he wills to do. It is this indubitable ability to act in accordance with one's past, that is glorified as the whole of freedom by those who call themselves determinists. They claim that this is all the liberty that a man could want, that a further degree of liberty would be scientifically false, metaphysically absurd, and ethically irrelevant. Now, as a libertarian and an indeterminist, I disagree most emphatically with this conception. I rejoice with the determinist that a person is determined by his own past and not solely, as a mechanistic fatalist would claim, by his external environment. It is better to be an embodied history, to possess a *durée réelle*, than just to be a particle, a puppet of fate. It is pleasant to be able to do as one desires, but it is not enough. In addition to my past and the shadows which it projects upon the future in the form of potentialities of imagination and anticipation, I want a living present, an indeterminate spontaneity that will enable me not merely to be myself and repeat myself, but to make of myself as I go something other and better than myself. I want, in short, a degree of liberty that will permit me not just

to do what I desire, but to do what I desire to desire,
what I know that I ought to desire.

That there does exist this extra element of freedom
I have no doubt. If the future were entirely and exclusively determined by the past, in each and every
aspect of its form and matter, it would be so perfect
a repetition of the past that it would be the past, and
time itself would not go on. There would be no Pas-
sage. The present contributes something new and vital
to the determination of the future. This is true of
everything, everywhere, a little. But in human life,
especially in moments of moral crisis, it is more than
true. It is at once the most significant and most certain of the deliverances of our experience. William
James was right when he said that the higher motives
are not the stronger motives, and that it is necessary
for us to throw the weight of our own free will into
the scales if we would make higher win over lower.
He was right also when he refused to let the determinist jockey him into the admission that the essence
of freedom lay in choosing between this motive and
that, as between being pulled to the left or being
pulled to the right. Such an admission is fatal for it
means that our selection of one motive rather than
another is either itself determined by a motive, which
is determinism, or else that the choice is motiveless
or reasonless, which would then be not our own work
but the work of mere chance, and, as such, void of
all moral significance. Freedom is, as James saw, the
freedom to make more or to make less of spontaneous
effort at the present moment to enact the higher

motive, the one that ought to win. There is no need of an ulterior motive for doing what we see to be good. It is in the effort that we will to make at the moment that our freedom consists. The amount of that effort is not predetermined by the past—it is determined spontaneously then and there in the present. I cannot, however, agree with James when he goes on to reduce all voluntary effort to effort of attention. There is a great deal of truth in the ideomotor theory but it does not explain all conscious action. A prospective act can be at the focus of attention without being willed and it can be willed without being at the focus of attention.

Thus, when the egoist declares that he is what he is and desires only what he desires, and can do no other I charge him with uttering a paradox and foully slandering the most clear and most precious part of his own being. For to say that you are what you are is none the less paradox and slander for being wrapped in the smug form of tautology. We are what we will to be at this present moment and not what we have been up to the present moment. In other words, we can create our future self, not of course entirely, but to a significant degree. External environment, including suggestion and exhortation of friends, together with past character and the slow, strong drag of habit, are indeed the complete determiners of the *form* and *content* of our desires and our motives. But whether we make the effort necessary to actualize the broader and higher of these desires and motives, or whether we lag and yield to the intrinsically stronger pull of our lower and narrower self, *that* is for us and us only, then, and then only, to decide.

The Relativity of Good and the Invariance of Virtue.

THE temper of life is fundamentally and incorrigibly heterodox; and never was there a worse misrepresentation than that involved in the classic definition of it as "the adjustment of inner to outer relations or situations." In this matter the biologists, even when anticlerical, have thoughtlessly followed the theological tradition, which was itself based upon a monarchical or patriarchal social psychology, in which obedience and conformity to external power was the end and measure of perfection in an individual. Yet here, as in many similar misrepresentations, there is the small fraction of truth that is necessary and sufficient to keep a fallacy alive and dangerous. Heterodoxy must have a modicum of orthodoxy in order to preserve itself from being crushed by the environment against which it contends. The living being must stoop to conquer. He must make his *ideas* conform to the facts of the world as a means of using his *ideals* to transform those facts.

Life is essentially an adventure; it informs its environment and thus transforms it. It treats objects as food for the actualization of its potentialities. It is an assimilator and an aggressor. The extent to which the aspirations of a living being are adjusted to its environment and made to conform to the world of things as they are, is not a measure of its degree of life, but rather of the degree to which it is already dead. Piety to the actual is impiety to the ideal. Accepting this as the central truth about life, we might seem to be committed to a complete relativity of values. For value is nothing alien or external to life; it is life itself viewed dynamically as growing or increasing its substance by actualizing its potentialities. For a thing to appear as a value means for it to appear as a promise of more life in some direction. This is not incompatible with the fact that death itself at times appears as a value. For as the suppression of one desire is often necessary for the fulfilment of other more important desires, so the destruction of an entire life system—it may be one's necessary prey, or it may be one's implacable foe, or it may even be one's own body—will, on occasion, be the only means of preserving a life, or some high phase of life that will, rightly or wrongly, appear more important than the life that is destroyed. The relativity of values that is implied by their being internal to life, and, in fact, consisting of its very substance, is reinforced by life's variability. Heretics are at variance not only with orthodoxy but with one another, and life not only grows at the expense of the environment but becomes more and more differentiated as it advances. The glory of life at the level attained by the human species is the uniqueness, actual or potential, of the persons composing that species. Any *régime* which would subordinate the individual and his liberties to that most insensate of all idols, the idol of the mass, whether political nation or economic class, goes directly counter to the whole nisus and genius of life.

It is not Communism or Fascism, but pure coöperative Anarchism that will characterize the golden age of the future, the loving and beloved community of completely free spirits.

This increasing differentiation of life that attends its increase in power, implies the relativity to individuals of all values, so far as their content or substance is concerned. One man's meat is another man's poison, and rules and customs that minister to progress at one phase of social development, may be criminally inappropriate and regressive at another. That is good, and that only, which helps any life in any situation, to actualize its potentialities.

In view of this utter relativity of values, and in view of the impossibility of finding an absolute criterion of value outside of life itself—in nature or supernature—it might seem that ethics could consist only of such limited universals as might be based on the similarities of individuals and their situations. There is, however, another way. When we say that nothing can dictate to life, we must be understood to mean *nothing except life itself*. The ideal of a maximum life emerges as the internal and autonomous absolute that replaces the external and heteronymous standards that we have rejected. Life seeks its own maximum, and the *summum bonum*, or supreme regulative criterion for values, is maximum abundance of life. Herein lies the autonomous but categorical imperative of Kantian memory. It is not, however, "the law that there shall be law" (which is Professor Palmer's felicitous interpretation of Kant's

principle) ; on the contrary, it is *the law that there
shall never be law,* but always a departure from law,
a maximum of variation, innovation, and adventure.
Life as thus conceived prescribes its own invariants,
two absolute virtues that shine steadily down upon
the flux of changing goods. They are invariant because they mark the road of maximum variation.
These two virtues are Love and Enthusiasm; they are
respectively the extensive and intensive coefficients
of life when most abundant; they are the two primary dimensions of righteousness.

Love, taken in its most inclusive sense, means
breadth and number of interests. The life that embodied it to the full would include in itself, through
sympathy, the desires, interests, and aims, the potentialities, in short, of all lives, present and future,
including its own. It would be at one with them in
their joys and pains and hopes and fears. The two
figures which history (in some ways clouded, and in
others clarified, by accretions of pious and tender
myth) presents to us as the highest earthly exem-
plars of this ideal, are Buddha and Christ. In Buddha
one finds the more universal sympathy, extending as
it does to brute as well as to human life. But the
completeness of Gautama's compassion is dimmed by
pessimism, and the Nirvana he would have us seek
is the abandonment of life rather than its perfection. In the teachings of Jesus we find, alas, no clear
word concerning animal suffering and our duty to
mitigate it. Yet the brutes who bleed and die for one
another and for us have no solace of religion or

philosophy to alleviate their agony, and their claim
for such sympathy and help as we can give should
be the more poignant and compelling from the very
fact that they are mute. Yet this strange and sad
exception to the gospel of universal pity need not
detract from the positive aspect of the Christ ideal,
which invites us not to abandon life and seek Nirvana, but to enhance, transfigure, and gloriously af-
firm it through mutual service.

And now for the second of our ethical invariants,
the virtue of "enthusiasm." I use the word for want
of a better to cover all that makes for the hard work
of actualizing potentialities. These do not actualize
themselves. They must be made actual by exercise
of will. An ideal merely in itself is like a bride; to
see her and yearn for her is a mockery unless it is
followed by the taking of her. Love is the "formal"
cause of righteousness; the capacity to behold ideals;
the "efficient" cause is enthusiasm, the energy to con-
summate them. Courage is the arch species of the
genus enthusiasm, for it is energy proving itself
under the duress of pain and the threat of pain.
Loyalty or steadfastness is closely related to courage,
for it is energy proving itself by cleaving to one's
chosen purpose against the lures and distractions of
others. But the energy to transform the ideal into
the real involves intelligence as well as courage and
singleness of heart. Cultivation of knowledge to the
end that it may be not only enjoyed as it should be,
but utilized as an increasingly effective instrument
for subduing the environment, and extending the

empire of spirit, is a duty, and one that is disclosed only to the modern eye. Neither Gautama, with his sympathy for all life, nor Jesus, with his flaming compassion for humanity, could realize the possibility of mastering the world without either abandoning or destroying it. The forces of evil were great and dark, and the power of secular intelligence was hardly visible. To Buddha, all individual life is poisoned at the source, and existence itself must be abandoned. For Jesus and his disciples the situation is less hopeless. Life itself could be saved and personality enhanced and perfected, but only by the destruction of this world and the creation of another. There was infinite courage, but it was the courage of despair, the strange flutelike courage of the weak in body to face death when exalted by spirit and its unearthly vision. But they did not know, and could not know, the kind of courage that has come to us, unworthy though we be, through science. Ours is the easy courage born of confidence and well-grounded hope. It is the reasoned faith that we can use the world if we cannot conquer it, and by harnessing the forces of nature to the demands of intelligence, transform an ancient foe into a patient friend and ally.

Enthusiasm must then, for any modern mind and in any truly modern ethics, include, along with the old-time courage of the heart, the new courage of the mind, the resoluteness to use intelligence to the limit in all dealings with our physical environment, our social institutions, and our own inmost selves.

There is yet another form of the virtue of enthusiasm which is essential to the attainment of the most abundant life. It is enthusiasm in the sense of concentrated intensity or abandon. The notion that Temperance possesses intrinsic moral value is as false as it is ancient and as mischievous as it is respectable. In all domains of primary or consummatory value there is an unrecognized but most important law, which, in contrast with the well-known economic law of diminishing returns, we may call the Law of Increasing Returns. It describes the fact that good and evil gain by concentration and lose by dispersion. A single great beauty is worth more than many pretties; a major poet is worth more than his own weight of minor poets; a supreme ecstasy cannot be equaled by a number of little joys. And on the side of negative value or evil it is the same. One tragic calamity embodies more misery than a number of small discomforts. It is less of an evil for many of us to suffer the slight annual pains of paying our insurance premiums than that any of us should suffer the real catastrophe of a great and irremediable loss. The miseries of a community should be dispersed and scattered as evenly as possible, for they are thereby lessened, and by the same token the goods should be combined into a comparatively small number of magnificent concentrations.

And as in a community so also in an individual. Given a certain prospective quantity of good and bad fortune the *optimum* distribution by which the good will be maximized and the bad minimized will be secured by intensive concentrations of positive values and extensive dispersions of those that are negative. From this it follows that the rule of temperance or the golden mean in matters of enjoyment is not wisdom but folly. The rewards of "plunging," "going the limit," "draining the cup to the last drop," etc., are out of all proportion greater than those of safe half-hearted dabbling on the principle of nothing too much. We should use temperance in our sins and sorrows, but when we are seeking not to escape from unhappiness but to achieve happiness for ourselves or others, enthusiasm in the sense of abandon or concentrated intensity should replace temperance as the rule of virtue and true wisdom.

There is in our country today a group of literary philosophers led by Mr. Irving Babbitt and Mr. Paul Elmer More. With somewhat questionable propriety they call themselves Humanists and their main purpose appears to be the undoing of the work usually associated with the name of Rousseau. They believe that human beings are not spontaneously good, that the impulses of the flesh are not to be trusted, and that an inner check, a *frein vital*, must be set up in definite opposition to the Old Adam or Natural Man in each of us. Mr. Walter Lippmann should, I think, be counted as an ally of the Humanists. Though starting from a more naturalistic metaphysics, he advocates a philosophy of conduct very similar to that of Mr. More and Mr. Babbitt. To all of these contemporary counter-revolutionaries the gospel of temperance, restraint, and self-control verging upon asceticism appeals as the only means of saving man-

kind from an orgy of anarchic self-indulgence and
rescuing human culture from a withering and materialistic decadence.

With some of the indictments brought by the Humanists I agree, but the corrective which they offer
appears to me unsound in theory and almost certainly futile in practice. The cure for the evils of
Rousseauism is not anti-Rousseauism but an exten-
sion and intensification of that great liberator's own
faith in the fulfilment of life by affirmation rather
than by negation. For better or worse life is utterly
committed to going forward. It is too late to retreat.
The spirit of man and his culture must win depth
and beauty and structural unity not by checking
its multitudinous potencies but by organizing them
around a single supreme devotion, the devotion to
securing a maximum pace of living for all who live.
No purely affirmative desire is bad, but some desires
are better than others. Sin consists only in preferring
the lesser to the greater good. In short, it is not more
temperance but more enthusiasm that is needed to
burn away the futilities, frivolities, and wastes that
plague us today.

The Relation of Religion to a Sanctionless Morality.

IT is my thesis that *true morality is without sanction*,
for sanctions are external justifications for righteousness and apologies for the good. That, in terms of
which every apology is given, itself needs no apology,
or rather, it is its own excuse for being. To make
religion the basis of morality, to make the obligation

to follow the better way, and to do the noble thing contingent upon the will of a God, is not only to degrade the nature both of morality and of religion, it is to put their very existence in jeopardy. It is the sin against the holy spirit, the spirit of man's higher self, which bids him choose what is beautiful and forego what is ugly in the conduct of his own life. Duty is nothing but the claim of the greater upon the lesser self. The doing of duty is the subordinating of the lesser good of the moment to that larger and more inclusive good comprising all the hopes and desires in ourselves and others. If we take any other reason or sanction for duty than that it involves the larger satisfaction of the larger self, it can mean only one thing, the justification of the higher and more inclusive interests of the person by some lower or narrower interest, such as fear of supernatural power. I do not deny that such a sanction may be practically effective. But while it is effective, and to the extent to which it is effective, the understanding of the good is obscured and morals are degraded through the subordination of right to might. Religion also is degraded, because if the validity of moral ideals depends on God's will, then God himself cannot be good unless there is some super-God to whose power *he* conforms—by such conformity earning the title of good. Unless the ideal of goodness is for God as for us, eternal in its own right, irrespective of anything in the world of existence, morality can have no ultimate significance.

Religion as the foundation of morality should be

abandoned, as indeed it is being abandoned. But there is still the possibility of a religion that should be the supplement and sequel to morality instead of its illegitimate and precarious basis. This is the religion that I call Promethean and it is the possibility of a Promethean religion that we are to consider in the next and concluding chapter.

III

GOD FINITE AND GOD INFINITE

IN our opening discussion we defined religion as the belief in a power greater than ourselves that makes for good. We defended this definition on the ground that it left religion free from the proven falsities, ethical and physical, embodied in traditional creeds, while at the same time it avoided the emptiness and platitude of those schools of ultra-modernism which cling to the word "religion," but use it to mean only the recognition of some sort of unity and mystery in the universe, plus a praiseworthy devotion to whatever is praiseworthy, as, for example, the perfecting of humanity. Taking religion as we took it, we see at once that it is neither certainly and obviously true nor certainly and obviously false, but possibly true, and, if true, tremendously exciting. The question of its truth or falsity is exciting and momentous because it is a question, not of the validity of this or that theory as to the nature of the physical world or as to the origin and destiny of the human race, but because it is the question whether the things we care for most are at the mercy of the things we care for least. If God is not, then the existence of all that is beautiful and in any sense good, is but the accidental and ineffective by-product of blindly swirling atoms, or of the equally unpurposeful, though more conceptually complicated, mechanisms of pres-

ent-day physics. A man may well believe that this
dreadful thing is true. But only the fool will say in
his heart that he is glad that it is true. For to wish
there should be no God is to wish that the things
which we love and strive to realize and make permanent, should be only temporary and doomed to frustration and destruction. If life and its fulfilments are
good, why should one rejoice at the news that God is
dead and that there is nothing in the whole world
except our frail and perishable selves that is concerned with anything that matters? Not that such a
prospect would diminish the duty to make the best
of what we have while we have it. Goodness is not
made less good by a lack of cosmic support for it.
Morality is sanctionless, and an ideal can never derive its validity from what is external to itself and to
the life whose fulfilment it is. Atheism leads not to
badness but only to an incurable sadness and loneli-
ness. For it is the nature of life everywhere to out-
grow its present and its past, and, in the life of man,
the spirit has outgrown the body on which it depends
and seeks an expansion which no finite fulfilment can
satisfy. It is this yearning for the infinite and the
sense of desolation attending the prospect of its
frustration that constitutes the motive to seek religion and to make wistful and diligent inquiry as to
the possibility of its truth.

The Prolegomena to Every Possible Theology.

THERE are two great problems which, taken together,
comprise the prolegomena to every possible theology

or atheology. They are the Problem of Evil and the Problem of Good.

How can the amount of evil and purposelessness in the world be compatible with the existence of a God? And how can the amount of goodness and purposefulness in the world be compatible with the nonexistence of a God?

1. *The Problem of Evil.* The first of these problems has already been touched upon, but its importance justifies us in considering it again. Of one thing we can be certain, since the existing world contains evil, God's alleged attributes of infinite power and perfect goodness can be reconciled only by altering the one or the other of those attributes. For surely it would seem that since God does not abolish evil it must be either because he can't or because he won't, which means that he is limited either in his power or in his goodness. The line more commonly adopted by theological apologetics is to preserve the infinite power of God at any cost and do what one can with the goodness. Since evil occurs, God must be willing that it should occur. Why? Well, perhaps evil is a mere negation or illusion; perhaps it is good in disguise, a necessary ingredient of divine satisfaction; or a desirable and natural punishment of human sin; or a lesson and opportunity for human good. Or God's ideal of goodness may be quite different from ours, etc. To each and all of these suggestions there are two answers, one theoretical, the other practical. In the theoretical retort we ask, if evil is only a negation or illusion or disguise, then

why should we and all other creatures suffer the failure to realize this? The experience of what is alleged to be unreal evil becomes itself the real evil. As for the portion of the world's evil that serves as a wholesome punishment or wholesome lesson for anybody, it is but an infinitesimal fraction of the total of the world's misery. Finally, if God's purposes are other than what we call good, then his nature is other than what we mean by good, while to go further and assume, as some absolute idealists have assumed, that our sin and agony actually contribute to God's enjoyment, would be to make him not merely lacking in good, but a demon of evil. In short, the explanations do not explain. But if they did (and this is the practical retort that follows and clinches the theoretical), the case of the theologians would be still worse; for if evil is really nothing, it is nothing to avoid; while if it is some disguised or indirect form of good, it is a duty to abet it, not oppose it. If the Vessels of Wrath, like the Vessels of Grace, contribute to the divine happiness, why should we care which sort of vessels our brothers and ourselves become? We should not only be "*willing* to be damned for the glory of God," we should strive for it. Surely no such vicious nonsense as that perpetrated by these defenders of God's unlimited power would ever have blackened the history of religious apologetics had it not been for man's ignoble and masochistic craving to have at any price a monarch or master, no matter how evil in the light of his own conscience such a master might be.

If our analysis of the Problem of Evil is valid, there can exist no omnipotent God. Possibly an omnipotent It, conceivably an omnipotent Demon, but not an omnipotent Goodness.

2. *The Problem of Good.* The world that we know contains a quantity of good which, though limited, is still far in excess of what could be expected in a purely mechanistic system.

If the Universe were composed entirely of a vast number of elementary entities, particles of matter or electricity, or pulses of radiant energy, which preserved themselves and pushed and pulled one another about according to merely physical laws, we should expect that they would occasionally agglutinate into unified structures, which in turn, though far less frequently, might combine to form structures still more complex, and so on. But that any considerable number of these higher aggregates would come about by mere chance would itself be a chance almost infinitely small. Moreover, there would be a steady tendency for such aggregates, as soon as they were formed, to break down and dissipate the matter and energy that had been concentrated in them. This increase of leveling, scattering, and disorganization to which all differentiated, concentrated, and organized aggregates are subject in our world, and in any world in which there is random motion alone, or random motion supplemented by such reciprocal *ab extra* determinations as are formulated in the laws of physics, is named the Increase of Entropy. This principle is exemplified in many familiar ways. The intense and concentrated waves caused by the stone dropped in the pool spread out and become less intense as their extensity increases. The hot stove in the cool room dissipates its differentiated and concentrated heat until a uniform level of temperature is reached. Stars radiate their energy and their mass into space, heavy and complex atoms break down into their simpler and lighter atomic constituents. Even the electrons and protons themselves are supposed to amalgamate and by so doing dissipate into space as short pulses of energy the very stuff of which they were made. And living organisms, with their minds, their societies, and their cultures, grow old, degenerate, and die, which is not merely the way of all flesh, but the way of all things.

And yet within this world that is forever dying, there have been born or somehow come to be, protons and electrons, atoms of hydrogen and helium, and the whole series of increasingly complex chemical elements culminating in radium and uranium. And these atoms not only gather loosely into nebulae, but in the course of time combine tightly into molecules, which in turn combine into the various complicated crystals and colloids that our senses can perceive. And on the only planet we really know, certain of the compounds of carbon gain the power of building themselves up by assimilation, and so growing and reproducing. Life thus started "evolves," as we say, into higher and higher forms, such as fishes, reptiles, and birds, mammals, primates, men, and, among men, sages and heroes.

Now the serious atheist must take his world seriously and seriously ask: What is the chance that all
this ascent is, in a universe of descent, the result of
chance? And of course by chance, as here used, we
mean not absence of any causality, but absence of
any causality except that recognized in physics. Thus
it would be "chance" if a bunch of little cards, each
with a letter printed on it, when thrown up into the
breeze, should fall so as to make a meaningful sen-
tence like "See the cat." Each movement of each
letter would be mechanically caused, but it would be
a chance and a real chance, though a small one, that
they would so fall. And if a sufficiently large bundle
of letters were thrown into the air there would also be
a chance that they would fall back so as to spell out
the entire play of Hamlet. The chance of this hap-
pening would be real enough, but it would be so small
that, if properly expressed as a fraction, $\frac{1}{n}$, the string
of digits contained in the denominator would, I suspect, reach from here to one of the fixed stars. And
as for the probability that the atoms composing the
brain of the author of Hamlet, if left to the mercy
of merely mechanistic breezes, would fall into the
combinations which that brain embodied—well, that
is a chance that is smaller still. Surely we need not
pursue the game further. Let the atheist lay the
wager and name the odds that he will demand of us.
Given the number of corpuscles, waves, or what not,
that compose the universe, he is to bet that with only
the types of mechanistic causality (or, if you are
modern and fussy about the word "cause" you can

call them "functional correlations") that are recognized in physics, there would result, I will not say the cosmos that we actually have, but any cosmos with an equal quantity of significant structures and processes. He certainly will not bet with us on even terms, and I am afraid that the odds that he will feel bound to ask of us will be so heavy that they will make him sheepish, because it is, after all, the truth of his own theory on which he is betting.

But what is the alternative to all this? Nothing so very terrible; merely the hypothesis that the kind of causality that we know best, the kind that we find in the only part of matter that we can experience directly and from within, the causality, in short, that operates in our lives and minds, is not an alien accident but an essential ingredient of the world that spawns us. The alternative to mere mechanistic determination is not some unknown thing concocted *ad hoc* to help us out of a difficulty. Surely, mind is a *vera causa* if ever there was one, and we merely suggest that the kind of anabolic and antientropic factor of whose existence we are certain in ourselves, is present and operative in varying degree in all nature. If we are right, we escape the universe of perpetual miracle, on which the atheist sets his heart. The organized structures and currents of ascent and evolution, from the atoms themselves to the lives of men, cease to be outrageously improbable runs of luck and become the normal expression of something akin to us. Material nature makes altogether too many winning throws for us not to suspect that she is playing with dice that are loaded, loaded with life and mind and purpose. This is the solution that seems to me almost inevitable of the problem which, for want of a better name, I have called the Problem of Good.

And so we are confronted with a God, or something very like a God, that exists, not as an omnipotent monarch, a giver of laws and punishments, but as an ascending force, a nisus, a thrust toward concentration, organization, and life. This power appears to labor slowly and under difficulties. We can liken it to a yeast that, through the aeons, pervades the chaos of matter and slowly leavens it with spirit.

The great difficulty of any theory of a finite God turns on his relation to the cosmic whole within which he functions. Legitimately or not, the mind rejects the kind of dualism involved. Moreover, a divine mind or personality can scarcely be conceived as other than a cosmic mind. It is, of course, possible that the earth, the solar system, or the galaxy to which we belong, has a unified consciousness associated with it, but no such limited system could be the body of God. Our interest in the problem of deity would not be satisfied by discovering a mind that was merely larger than our own. Nor would any such limited mind throw light upon the antientropic factor which we have accepted as a finite God, and which, despite its finitude, appears to pervade the entire cosmos and hence to indicate a relationship to the totality different from and more intimate than that of a part to its whole. Are we then forced to conclude that the finite God, which solved for us the Problem of Good, requires as correlate the infinite God of religious tradition who seemed to be precluded by the Problem of Evil?

The Relation of Mind and Matter.

BEFORE facing this question directly let us consider the conception of a cosmic mind, and attempt to discover whether the meager evidence that is available makes for or against the validity of the conception. That at least one form of matter is most intimately involved with mind we know by the incontrovertible evidence of our own experience. If no other matter in the universe has mind, at least the matter composing human brains does certainly possess it. Now the stuff of our brains is different from other stuff, but not so very different. It is made of the same sort of atoms which are subject to the same laws as are found in matter generally. The organization of the stuff is, to be sure, markedly different from inorganic organizations, and markedly more intricate than those found in lower forms of life. But even here the gap is not too great for evolution or descent to bridge. Men and their kings have developed from simpler organizations than those of cabbages, and presumably the ultimate ancestors of all living beings were not properly ancestors at all, for they were the non-vital, or pre-vital, aggregations from which the first life emerged.

I cannot myself believe for one instant that a difference so finite and relative as that between man's body and the inorganic dust from which it came, could adequately measure the infinite and absolute difference between conscious and non-conscious being. To suppose that a mere rearrangement of the same chemical atoms could create out of nothing a whole new dimension of reality, such as feeling or consciousness, seems to me beyond the limits of possibility. If sentience is based on matter it cannot be based merely upon some special distribution of its particles, it must rather be intrinsic to material being as such. Once this panpsychist postulate is accepted, then indeed we can with comparative ease go on to impute and apportion differences of the sentient systems to the differences of their physical organization.

Life as we know it is confined to the highly specialized colloidal jelly called protoplasm; and rational or personal life is confined to the still more highly specialized forms of that jelly exemplified in the human cerebrum and its connections. When we scan the universe with our telescopes we find galaxy after galaxy sprawling through a space that, if not infinite and without all structure, is at least destitute of anything that in the least resembles the structure of a brain and sense organs as we know them. I shall not attempt to prove with any approach to convincing detail that the conception of the cosmos as a living organism is true. I wish only to present certain considerations which I regard as important in themselves and as constituting a preface to such a proof.

Every existent thing possesses two kinds of being, "actual" and "potential." Its *actual* being is what it overtly is at any given place in any given instant, a group of qualities primary and relational alone, or primary and secondary, with a date and a locus, capable of being externally observed, by a properly situated observer. Its *potential* being is private or internal, and not capable of appearing externally. The simplest or lowest form of potentiality is the capacity to be or repeat itself through the succession of instants that constitutes time. Such would be the potentiality of an unchanging material substance, a continuous history or "world line" of the same qualities through a series of instants. But as motion or change of spatial position is relative to a frame of reference, and as all things are in motion in all frames but their own, we should include uniform motion along with rest, and define this lowest level of potentialities as the capacity of a thing to be not merely in another instant in time but in another *point-instant* of *space-time* than the one in which it actually is here and now. Non-uniform or accelerated motion and motions having accelerations of accelerations, etc., will be the successively higher degrees of potentiality and will be attended by change of qualities as well as change of position. Everything except a shadow or a negation of matter would have at least the lowest grade of potentiality; and as we ascend from mere waves of radiant energy through protons and electrons to the atomic molecular and intermolecular organizations, there will be higher and more complex systems of potential energy associated with the increasingly complex actualities of material structure. It would seem that it was not until we reached the degree and type of complexity that is represented by protoplasm that the potentialities of a thing attained a critical point, a point where they could not only preserve themselves, but *spread* themselves or *impose* themselves upon other systems. It is by a kind of transfer analogous to electrostatic induction, that the pattern of forces or potentialities in a living cell imposes parts of itself upon the food particles brought within its field, and so grows by anabolizing and assimilating them. And when the whole pattern and not merely part of it is induced in, or imposed upon, other matter, there is reproduction, and the new units thus brought into being grow and reproduce in their turn, distributively in the unicellular organisms, and collectively as well as distributively in the multicellular. And so life spreads and ramifies and evolves into systems of higher, deeper, and richer potentialities until the comparatively meager system of atoms composing the fertilized cell from which a multicellular organism is to grow, contains hidden in itself, in an intensive hierarchy, the unimaginably multitudinous potentialities which are at once the register of millions of generations of past ancestry and the determinants of the gestation or ontogeny of the new individual, which in turn contains the seed of further progeny in the future.

In treating of this matter before, we advanced the theory that the animal mind, and the nervous system associated with it, was an organism within an organism, a new level of life and a new type of life system. The body as a whole takes in energy only when mixed with matter, but the brain takes its energy *neat;* and that pure energy, composed of the specific forms of motion that come over the nerves to the cerebrum, leaves traces there which are retained and assimilated into a memory system or private history. By the animal mind as thus constituted the animal guides his reactions to the here and now by the consciousness of events distant in time and space. He profits by his past and anticipates his future. In the long course of evolution there came a time when this secondary system of potentialities pertaining to the special life of the brain attained sufficient strength to function with a certain independence, and not merely as an instrument to the sensory and motor exigencies of the bodily situation. It was then that the animal became man. The mind of man has power to contemplate the past and imagine the future, and to use the body and its environment as a means to the fulfilment and development of its ideals. Mind when thus emancipated, autonomous and dominant, is *spirit*. Man is a spirit for he rules the soil in which he grows. The place and the time of his life on earth is the place and the time of his body, but the meaning and the value of even his earthly life is as eternal and as beautiful as he wills to make it.

The cosmic evolution that has been so hastily sketched possesses one general characteristic to which I would call special attention. Central and crucial in the whole process is the steady increase of the form of being which we call potential, the private and not externally observable phase of a thing which is both the history of its past and the determiner of its future. Anything that is in any kind of process, even the process of continuing its own identity, has that about it at each present instant which we from outside can only describe by the justly unpopular, vague, and negative term "potentiality." Now there can be no such thing as a mere potentiality. The potentiality of a future chicken is something actual in the present egg. The potentiality of anything that was or will be must in some sense itself be both present and actual, not physically or externally actual and present, but yet somehow real there and then in the thing itself. There is, however, only one thing conceivable that can qualify to give present actuality to the future and the past, and that is *consciousness*. For consciousness is the vicarious presence at a given place and time of events which, in their own right, occupy other places and times. What we from without refer to as a thing's *potentialities* is from within, and for itself, the content of that thing's *consciousness*. And as consciousness is the only actuality that can give specific and intrinsic meaning to material potentiality, so conversely the only possible way in which consciousness can be really present in the physical world and really operative in physical things is as the potentialities of those things. Potentiality and consciousness are alike in being real but private, present here and now, yet constituted of what is there and then. This, which I hold to be a most fundamental metaphysical truth, is not generally recognized, partly because *the word "potentiality" ex-*

presses only one part of its own intent. From the essentially pragmatic standpoint of an external observer, the hidden aspect of a thing can be admitted only as what will appear as its *future,* for it is only the future that we shall be able to observe. But the real basis of the thing's future is its past and for the thing itself that past, or history, would be the content of its potentiality, i.e., the content of its consciousness. This becomes clear when we change our standpoint from the outer to the inner and view directly our own potentialities rather than indirectly those of others. Then we find that it is the duration of the past in the present that is the primary stuff of our experience and that our anticipation of the future is the quite secondary and mediated adaptation of that. We only experience that which already is, and what already is, is what was. Herein lies the significance of the etymology of the word "fact." A fact is a *factum,* something that now is done, a *fait accompli.* And nothing can enter consciousness without this touch of retrospection that characterizes fact. In short, though we live forward into the future, we experience backward into the past. To the external observer it is the future actions which are of interest, because he will be able to perceive them, so he names the inner life of a thing its potentiality. But the true inner nature of anything, its self-transcending reference to what is not itself, faces two ways, into the future and into the past. "Potentiality" is the most available single word for it, but that word ordinarily connotes but one aspect and that one which for the thing itself is least significant. This I think is the reason why, at first hearing, my theory will sound strange to you—the theory, namely, that *the potentiality of being is the sentience of being*, and that as potentiality is ubiquitous and omnipresent so therefore is consciousness.

The Question of a Cosmic Mind.

IF the arguments that I have advanced are valid, it follows that the great question of whether the totality of material elements that make up the universe is the bearer of a unitary life and mind is not to be decided by the absence of structures that resemble the organisms that we know. What qualifies a material system to be the bearer of spirit is not hands or eyes or brain. It is, first, *the organization of its components into a single system*, and, second, *the capacity of that system to retain its past as a living present history and to possess the potentialities of future change commensurate with that history*. Now, however perishable the parts of the universe may be, the whole itself is enduring, and nothing happens without leaving its trace; while as for the unity of the cosmos, it would seem that the very fact that it is self-contained, with nothing beyond into which it can scatter, would confer upon it a higher degree of organicity than would be possible for any system included within it.

It is perhaps at this point in the discussion that the pantheist will warn us not to ascribe personality to whatever of unitary mind and life the world as a whole may be supposed to possess. With an impres-

sive assumption of piety, he will tell us that persons
are finite, and that it would be an insult to God to
impute to him an attribute so characteristic of human
limitation. It seems to me that the piety of the pantheist is distorted and mistaken. A mind gains personality through gaining a more perfect, intimate,
and articulate *rapport* among its elements, and an
emancipation from the status of body servant. Personality is mind become substantive and autonomous,
mind become spirit. If the universe has a mind, that
mind would be more rather than less personal than
ours, for it would have more rather than less of unity
and organicity. Yet there is one element in the pantheistic conception of personality which I believe to
be sound. A *person* must have an *environment* with
which he is in interaction. Now, how can the mind of
the universe, outside of which there can be nothing,
possess an environment? The answer seems to me
plain. If we are not frightened by the etymology of
the term, we can speak of an "internal environment."
"That in God which is not God" is God's environment, and *that* is the "world." The world consists of
all finite existences, energies, particles, or what not.
Each has its inner, or mental, potentialities, and its
outer, or material, actuality, and each has its measure
of self-affirming spontaneity or primary causality,
and also its inertia or passivity by which it figures as
a term in the network of predominantly mechanistic
interrelations. One is here tempted to distinguish the
world mind from the world by using the old phrases
natura naturans and *natura naturata*, but the temp-

tation must be resisted, for *natura naturata* is tainted
with the pantheistic exaltation of the whole at the
expense of the parts which are then no longer parts
but mere phases or "modes" of a one and only "Substance." Now, the real things of the real world are
things in their own right, active and obstreperous
entities, constituting a modified mechanism which,
with respect to values, is a good deal of a chaos. This
chaos, however, as we have seen, appears to be under-
going an amelioration genuine though painfully slow,
and the leaven that works in it, and by which its
evolution is wrought, we called the finite God.

The Finite Will of an Infinite God.

How is the unitary and personal yet infinite cosmic
consciousness related to the finite God that is the
cosmic nisus? Surely there are not two Gods, the one
an Invisible King, the other a sort of Captain Cou-
rageous! Their relation is rather that of a mind to
its will—a will of finite power working within the
confines of an infinitely extended and all-inclusive
mind. God, as thus conceived, is a *self* struggling to
inform and assimilate the recalcitrant members of
his own organism or the recalcitrant thoughts of his
own intellect. For each organic member or each con-
stituent thought has a being and life of its own, like
that of the whole of which it is a part. The purpose
and value sought by the Great Life is the same as
that of the lesser lives within; no fixed *telos* or *end*,
but a maximum increase of life itself. Not merely or
primarily an increase in the number of all lives, but

rather a greater enrichment, enhancement, and expansion of each life. For God as for us all, goods are relative, variable, and growing. New values are generated by old, and new summits of beauty are revealed from the summits already ascended. But also it is true that for God, as for us, the form of good remains constant through the flux of content. Life absolute and life relative create their own unchanging way to their own unlimited growth—the twofold way of virtue, an ever more intensive *enthusiasm* and an ever more extensive *love*. Life's own and only goal is infinite and unending increase.

The New Worldliness.

FROM abstract and speculative theology let us turn to concrete religion and its possible place in human experience. And here we are confronted with a new problem quite different from those that we have so far considered. Man's first gods were children of fear, fear which was itself the offspring of a more than animal power to anticipate the dangers of nature united with an all but animal weakness in coping with them. Gradually this weakness was transformed into strength, and magic, the first false dawn of intelligence, gave way to real though primitive science. Man learned to tame the animals, to sow the soil, to fight and build with tools, and from the early gods of fear there slowly came the God of sorrow. Humanity had gained some respite from the cruder plagues of material nature, and turning its attention inward, began to note the failures and tragedies of life, its griefs and sins. Mere physical terror was mitigated and supplemented by pity, and self-pity, and shame. The new God and his Other World became the solace, precious and irreplaceable, for all who were cast down. Religion, and it alone, could function as a sustaining vital force in men who saw that death would come to them, and who believed their very world would also die.

Now times are changed. Humanity, though not exactly come of age, has reached its adolescence and in a new, and for the most part, buoyant mood, would put all childish things away, and among them its old religion. It was this Modern Temper that was the theme of our opening discussion. We considered its indictment of religion both on the ground of its alleged historic, scientific, and metaphysical falsities, and on the ground of its alleged evil and reactionary philosophy of morals. But there is a third indictment which we did not consider but which is perhaps the most dangerous because the most practically influential of all. It is the indictment that is based on the increasing *irrelevance* of religion to the needs and interests of modern life. That this challenge, though less vocal than the others, is more deadly, will be apparent when we remember that true things can survive the charge of falsity and good things thrive under the charge of evil, but nothing however good or true can endure as a living force in an atmosphere of indifference and neglect.

To the modern temper religion is fast coming to seem unnecessary because fear and sorrow are no longer the major themes of our more serious culture. There is a *new worldliness* that is the outcome, not of thoughtlessness and triviality, but of a new thoughtfulness and a new confidence in man's power to make life happy and secure by purely secular devices. Already we have the means to conquer poverty and to supply all the necessities and an increasing number of luxuries to every member of a sanely controlled population. The time is almost here when, learning our lesson from Malthus, we shall break through the cobwebs of obscurantism and superstition and emancipate our species from the stupidest, oldest, and most shameful of all slaveries—the slavery to its own overproduction. And when once the quality of life is no longer surrendered to its quantity, not even the ineptitudes of an economy based purely on private profit can delay for more than a few years the permanent solution of the problem of poverty and a permanent recovery from the insanity of war.

Let us go on from the conquests of poverty and of war to the less assured but still measurably probable conquests of secular intelligence in the more remote future. Diseases of the body and disorders of the mind and emotions may be definitely eliminated, and it is conceivable that life itself may be indefinitely prolonged. A mastery of the glands may yield anodynes not merely for physical pains but for the miseries of cowardice, jealousy, and hate, and of all moral and intellectual sloth. We may even succeed in not only controlling the quantity of life, but in eugenically directing its quality along new and ever higher lines of our own choosing. With the keys to birth and death in their hands, directors of their own evolving destiny, it would only remain for these supermen of the future to preserve their new life from geologic and astronomic catastrophes, and, last of all, from the relentless increase of entropy and its *dénouement* in a dissolution of the whole material universe into unavailable waves of energy. Let us give to our improbable supermen the more than improbable, yet less than impossible, power which they will some day surely need. And to the younger Haldane's brilliant gifts, synthetic foods and psychic anodynes, ectogenesis and self-directed evolution, along with the power to migrate to other planets, stars, and galaxies, let us add one final gift—the best of all. We will reincarnate Clerke Maxwell's famous "Demon" and confer upon our progeny the power to reverse the downward flow of energy, and to make not only synthetic food, but synthetic matter. By their own Utopian alchemy they will take the end products of entropy, the degraded energies left from dead and dying worlds, and transmute them into electrons and protons and all their higher atomic products to satisfy whatever needs they may have.

Then, and only then, would mortal flesh have put on immortality and both individual and collective life have won true lordship over all creation.

Now the purpose of this journey to the further frontiers of Utopia is not to weigh the probabilities or appraise the advantages of the earthly life to come. It is not the truth of the dream, but the fact

of the dream, that is of interest to us. Dreams like
this are being dreamt today, and whether well or ill
grounded, they are significantly diagnostic of that
phase of the modern temper which will make it difficult for the religions of old to continue. Religion has
been a defense against fear and a flight from sorrow.
To the extent that men see a prospect of abolishing,
or radically mitigating, these enemies of their happiness, they will reject the technique of escape and its
mood of defeatism. Religion will be *outmoded,* and
its tidings of escape to another and better world will
ring cold in the ears of those who love this. The new
worldliness that religion must face is based on the
faith that there is not only no *place* for heaven, but
no *need* for it. Humanity, adolescent at last, has
tasted the first fruits of the victory of secular intelligence over nature, and dreams grandly of far greater
victories to come.

How then can the spirit of religion meet this new
challenge? There is, as I see it, but one course to take.
The traditional religious orientation toward life and
its values must undergo a revolutionary revision.
The alternative to this revolution is not quick death
for religion at the hands of brave atheists, but slow
death from neglect by a world that will have passed
it by.

A Preface to Promethean Religion.

THE myth of Prometheus was made in Hellas, dis-
tilled from the purest and best in the souls of Greeks.
Though its setting is local and temporal, its lesson

is universal and eternal; and among all the allegories of all the peoples it stands supreme.

We can take it as a translation of the Hebrew epic of Job into the terms of a happier, freer, and more worldly culture; and the outcome in the one case is significantly different from that in the other. Both of the heroes, actuated by love and justice, pledge their loyalty to the ideal and to it alone, and by that very fact they anger and alarm the gods of things as they are. Both are punished for their righteousness, and then the stories diverge. Job yields at last and surrenders right to might. Prometheus endures the tyrant's torture and keeps his spirit free, proclaiming to gods and men alike the claim of the ideal to outrank the power of Heaven itself. There is a second difference between the Greek and the Hebrew heroes. Job was righteous, but necessarily in a small way; being human, he lacked the far-flung vision of a demigod. Prometheus not only defied the real in the interest of the ideal, but the ideal for which he suffered was that of progress on earth for men. Progress not by submission, but by intelligence; secular progress which, like the knowledge of good and evil, had been the prerogative of the gods alone. The fire that Prometheus stole from Heaven to give to men was the symbol of just that priceless thing. And one must suppose that when, after a long season, Plato was born, it was Prometheus and not Apollo who was his real father. For as Prometheus was first among the immortals to proclaim the two great truths, supremacy of the ideal and the power of free intelligence, so was that Philosopher who has no peer, the first among mortals to proclaim those same two truths; a realm of eternal ideals whose beauty no fact can dim and no force subdue, and to whose validity the gods themselves must bow, and secondly, the duty and the power of men to make over their own institutional life by the revolutionary use of reason, and to build an ideal Republic.

There is desperate need to adapt our religion to the spirit and mood of the Promethean myth, and to make of it in a very real sense a Promethean religion. For the Promethean temper is the modern temper at its best, and best expresses the present vision of what man's life should be, and what, if things go well, it actually will become.

Fortunately, the task is not so difficult as it might seem, for it is tradition only, and not truth, that stands in the way. If God is, as I believe he is, an infinite, all-inclusive cosmic life, whose will to good is single, pure, and finite, one force among many in that chaos of existence which God finds within himself and which is the world he would perfect—if God is that, then Zeus and his cousin of old Judea never were at all except as nightmare dreams in the minds of their worshipers. It was Prometheus himself, not Zeus, who all along was really God, or the Hellenic symbol of what Christians name the Holy Ghost.

Religious experience at its highest and deepest would be the contact which mortal men might have with immortal spirit, the Holy Spirit of God that sweeps like a wind through chaos, and forms all material structures—the electrons, atoms, and molecules, and their aggregates, the nebulae stars and planets, and the living bodies of human beings. Surely it is not too fantastic to believe that a spirit that is everywhere can also be here, and on occasion visit mortals and make known its presence in their hearts: when they are in sorrow, as a comforter; when they are bewildered, as a light; when they are in terror, as a power; when they are in joy, as a glory.

It has at any rate been often so reported. And these reports and testimonies should be in the future, as after all they always have been, the primary source of all religion. Mythology and metaphysics and their various combinations in the many rational and revealed theologies can never do more than serve as the more or less dead frames of what is felt to be by those who have it, be they saints, messiahs, or ordinary folk, a living contact with something other and infinitely higher than themselves.

But now for the moment let us put quite out of our minds the question of whether these contacts occur, and of whether the mystic visit of the soul of the whole to the soul of the part is a fact or an illusion. And let us ask only whether such visits, even if they had occurred and even if they were still possible, would be any longer welcome in a world in which man is coming into his own and dreaming Utopian dreams of secular conquest and of an earthly future when pain and sadness and weakness will be no longer the determining factors in his spiritual orientation.

There is certainly today a rapidly increasing num-

ber of those who in answer to this question would
unhesitatingly demand a severing of all connections,
real or apparent, between man and the supernatural.
Of course all, or almost all of them, will hasten to
add that in reality there never had been and never
could be any such connections. But in that part of
their reply we are not now interested. It is not their
belief in the falsity of religion but only their belief
in its present and future irrelevancy that concerns
us. Are the new worldlings right in their ethics of
naturalism and atheism? It is that that we must seriously consider. We must suppose them to amplify
their thesis as follows: "Fear and ignorance made the
old gods—and in a world of ignorance and fear, that
was right enough, though of course there weren't any
gods there. Sorrow and failure and sin made the
Great God, and that was all right too. For though
there wasn't any such being, yet in the presence of
an invincible enemy techniques of flight and surren-
der are justifiable. But now that the enemy is in
retreat and our permanent happiness in a fair way
to be secured, no sort of god is wanted, not even if
he existed. Religion is defeatism both shameful and
unnecessary. It will go, must go, and ought to go.
'Salvation' is an anachronism, for there is nothing to
be saved *from*. We shall gain the whole world and—
be sufficient unto ourselves."

This is the modern temper; this is what religion
is up against. How shall we reply? After all, the root
of the answer is old. The living God, we are told, is
adequate to man and needed by him in good fortune

as in bad. But is he? That is the whole point. The early gods were, to be sure, invited to feasts and made really welcome. And even now, at many tables, grace is still said, though it is apt to be followed by an odd little sigh of relief when it is over, and we can begin. Of course there is the story of one who was welcomed to a wedding feast and who turned water into wine, but that story has been put on the Puritan Index and to refer to it at a Dry dinner would be the height of bad form. But what is more significant and disconcerting, the same reference would be a little embarrassing even at a Wet dinner. It would elicit a polite and perfunctory approval, but the subject of conversation would be quickly changed. We must remember that the Puritans, from Paul to Torquemada and from Calvin to Anthony Comstock, have succeeded in impressing their own conception of religion not merely upon their friends, but even upon their foes. God as help in time of trouble? Yes. But at other times it is God as punisher, prohibitor, censor, kill-joy—relentless foe of worldly life.

Now man today has pretty finally accepted this world, not, we must hope, as a norm of values, but as his place of operation and his permanent home. He is committed to it and to its improvement; and the great techniques of other-worldliness are dying and will soon be dead. The prerequisite to any genuine revival of religion is not therapy but surgery, not evolution but revolution. Authoritarianism and Asceticism are the twin cancers of Puritanism. They have poisoned religion even in its ministry to failure and pain, and on that account alone they should be cut out with all their roots and ramifications. If these things can once be made to go, I believe that there is hope. For that which tainted the old religion is also the chief obstacle to the continuance of any form of religion in the future.

Nobody will deny that man is finite, and will continue finite no matter how many continents he may tame, or how many planets he may colonize, or how many atoms he may disintegrate and reintegrate. Pain, fear, and misery he may abolish, but the finitude of his being he will not abolish. Yet for better or worse there is associated with this finitude a longing for the infinite. Though finite, man needs the infinite to complete and unify his own being. His spirit has pathetically outgrown his flesh, even his Utopian flesh. That is the mystery and the paradox of our natures. It is obvious enough that this need should be felt most poignantly in moments of weakness and failure. Men drowning clutch even at straws. The real test of our strange need will come when we are prosperous, not temporarily prosperous, as in the past, for then it was but natural and prudent to be on the safe side, but when we are permanently prosperous, when we arrive safe in Utopia; or if that arrival seems dubious—and it assuredly is, all wild fancies to the contrary notwithstanding—then when we dream, as assuredly we now do dream, that we are on the way to Utopia.

In the theory of value defended in the second chapter, the good was defined as the increment of psychic being which constitutes the actualization of a potentiality. If the definition was sound and if it is true that we have a need or potentiality for contact with the infinite, then the actuality of such contact should be a tremendous thing, an infinite addition to what there is of us. Why should anyone refuse it, if it were really possible to have it? One might indeed, in times of good fortune, forget it; one might even allow the instinct for it to atrophy through disuse and neglect, and cease to care for aught but finite goods so long as they were supplied in plenty. But could anyone deny that the loss would be real and, indeed, more terribly real if the very desire itself were lost and not merely the fulfilment of it? The self would have actually been diminished in its possible substance, something would have dropped out of the prospect and that something the infinite. If we were right in pitying the egoist for lacking sympathies and being so small in that very thing that he was exclusively concerned for, namely, his own self, is not the same sort of pity to be given to the atheist who, having the opportunity to enlarge his life by contact with the infinite, neglected that opportunity? Not that anything would happen to him—his tragedy would consist just in that—in the fact that nothing would happen to him. He would keep right on being himself, but nothing more. He would have lost nothing that he had, only something that he could have had—an infinite something. And let us remember here the Promethean conception of God that was defended. If that conception is valid it means that the holy spirit of God, could one but feel it, would not only be courage to hearten us in weakness, and solace to comfort us in sorrow (perhaps in Utopia we are not ever weak or sad), but power and light and glory beyond what we had, however much we had. No one would knowingly refuse that, even in Utopia. For though life may lose its negations and evils, so long as life continues as life, it will never lose its yearning to be more than it is. The Promethean God, unlike the old God of evil tradition, would be life-affirming, not life-negating; he would not pull us back from our interests and recall us from the world. We should be lifted up and carried forward, as by a wave, further into the world and its life than before, our interests broadened and deepened and our souls miraculously quickened.

If that is in truth what an authentic religious experience would mean or could mean, then for those who object to religion there remains but one possible line—they must deny that there is such a thing. Of course it would be good, they will say, if it were real, but it is not real; it is but a revival of ancient empty hope masking its emptiness in phrases. Abandon it and let us give what time and energy we have to our real business of living like mortals in a world which none but mortals inhabit. To this we can only reply: Perhaps you are right, but there is a chance that you are not. There is at least a chance that there is an upward-tending power in nature to account for such adaptations as we find. There is at least a chance that the cosmos as a whole has a unitary life and consciousness and that the evolutionary nisus is its will which, though not omnipotent, is omnipresent. And lastly, if there is a kind of stillness and if one can contrive a queer little turn of the heart away from what one knows to be mean, there is a chance, however small, that a union with the holy spirit of this Promethean God will be attained, and that by such union, one's world will be made radiant, and one's life become a high romance.

THE
DWIGHT HARRINGTON TERRY
FOUNDATION

LECTURES ON RELIGION
IN THE LIGHT OF
SCIENCE AND PHILOSOPHY

THE accompanying volume is based upon the seventh series of lectures delivered at Yale University on the Foundation established by the late Dwight H. Terry of Plymouth, Connecticut, through his gift of $100,000 as an endowment fund for the delivery and subsequent publication of "Lectures on Religion in the Light of Science and Philosophy."

The deed of gift declares that "the object of this Foundation is not the promotion of scientific investigation and discovery, but rather the

The Dwight Harrington Terry Foundation Lectures

·.·

Belief Unbound

·.·

Wm. Pepperell Montague

assimilation and interpretation of that which has been or shall be hereafter discovered, and its application to human welfare, especially by the building of the truths of science and philosophy into the structure of a broadened and purified religion. The founder believes that such a religion will greatly stimulate intelligent effort for the improvement of human conditions and the advancement of the race in strength and excellence of character. To this end it is desired that lectures or a series of lectures be given by men eminent in their respective departments, on ethics, the history of civilization and religion, biblical research, all sciences and branches of knowledge which have an important bearing on the subject, all the great laws of nature, especially of evolution . . . also such interpretations of literature and sociology as are in accord with the spirit of this Foundation, to the end that the Christian spirit may be nurtured in the fullest light of the world's knowledge and that mankind may be helped to attain its highest possible welfare and happiness upon this earth . . .

"The lecturers shall be subject to no philosophical or religious test and no one who is an earnest seeker after truth shall be excluded because his views seem radical or destructive of existing beliefs. The founder realizes that the liberalism of one generation is often conservatism in the next, and that many an apostle of true liberty has suffered martyrdom at the hands of the orthodox. He therefore lays special emphasis on complete freedom of utterance, and would welcome expressions of conviction from sincere thinkers of differing standpoints even when these may run counter to the generally accepted views of the day. The founder stipulates only that the managers of the fund shall be satisfied that the lecturers are well qualified for their work and are in harmony with the cardinal principles of the Foundation, which are loyalty to the truth, lead where it will, and devotion to human welfare."

The
Dwight
Harrington
Terry
Foundation
Lectures
∴
Belief
Unbound
∴
Wm.
Pepperell
Montague

At the Printing-Office of the Yale University Press.